HOW TO
SEARCH
THE
SCRIPTURES

HOW TO
SEARCH
THE
SCRIPTURES

Dr. Fuchsia Pickett

CREATION
HOUSE

HOW TO SEARCH THE SCRIPTURES by Fuchsia Pickett
Published by Creation House
Strang Communications Company
600 Rinehart Road
Lake Mary, Florida 32746
Web site: http://www.creationhouse.com

Unless otherwise noted, all Scripture quotations are from the
King James Version of the Bible.

Library of Congress Cataloging-in-Publication Data
How to search the scriptures / Fuchsia Pickett.
    p.   cm.
ISBN: 0-88419-587-2 (pb)
    1. Bible—Study and teaching. I. Title.
BS600.2.P489 1999
220'.071—dc21   98-53968
                                                        CIP

9 0 1 2 3 4 5 6 BBG 8 7 6 5 4 3 2 1
Printed in the United States of America

Contents

Foreword

In partnership with *SpiritLed Woman* magazine, Creation House has developed the SpiritLed Woman imprint, designed to publish women's books that will encourage women to mature spiritually. Creation House now has its first SpiritLed Woman books available. Developed to help women study the Word of God, these first study books have been written by Dr. Fuchsia Pickett, who has been a seminary professor and Bible teacher for many years. She brings fresh revelational insights from Scripture that will change your life as you apply their truth. Dr. Pickett has had a tremendous impact on me personally, and I recommend her work wholeheartedly.

This four-book series includes the full-length, foundational study titled *How to Search the Scriptures.* This volume will provide you with the tools for in-depth Bible study of God's Word. It outlines several methods of Bible study, including synthetic and inductive methods of study as well as study by topics, types, or biographies. This volume will become an invaluable tool for any future Bible study you may do.

The first three study guides *SpiritLed Woman* has

chosen to present to you are studies on the lives of Deborah, Esther, and Ruth. These three women represent the truly SpiritLed woman, moving from ancient Bible days into the twenty-first century—giving us role models by which we can learn to be SpiritLed women of today.

Deborah, the first of these studies, takes a look at one of the Bible's most courageous women. She filled the position of prophet and judge of Israel during a twenty-year period of captivity by the Canaanites. In this study you will learn how one woman, in obedience to the Spirit of God, not only led a nation, but actually became a deliverer for the people of God.

The prophetic message contained in the story of Esther, our second powerful woman, reveals the "church within the church." As you study the life of Esther through allegory and type, you will explore deep truths concerning your relationship with God, individually and corporately, and His plan for the church. This is a fascinating study of the relentless war for final supremacy that is being waged within the soul of man between good and evil.

Then as you study the allegorical, historical love story of our third SpiritLed woman, Ruth, you will see her pivotal position in the genealogy of the house of David and of Jesus Christ. Through her relationship with Naomi and Boaz, you will gain fresh insights about your own relationship with God.

I pray that God will open the eyes of your spiritual understanding as a result of the time you spend with these Bible studies. Accept the challenge and rise up to be a SpiritLed woman!

—JOY STRANG, PUBLISHER
SPIRITLED WOMAN

Foreword

There is no woman of God more worthy of honor than Dr. Fuchsia Pickett. As a teacher, she exhibits the highest standards of biblical scholarship and spiritual integrity. Over the years, she has paid the price for many of the benefits we enjoy today as women who preach and teach God's Word. She has mentored (and mothered) thousands of us, and her legacy among saintly women *and men* is great.

How to Search the Scriptures is an invitation to explore the foundational tenets of our faith in God and knowledge of His Word. In times such as these in which we live, it's vital to know what we believe, in whom we believe, and why.

When I first met Dr. Pickett some years ago, I was amazed by the confidence and grace with which she opened and served the "bread" of God's Word. Today, she still has a knack for unfolding spiritual truth that makes you wonder how you could have "missed it" for so long and why you never saw it that way before.

Her passion for God, so conspicuous in her writings, has inspired and challenged me many times. I want to know and love Jesus as she does. But I sense it will take all of eternity for me to even begin to catch up.

In surveying the riches of the Word of God, she is way out in front of most of us. We could never ask for a more accomplished and capable guide.

The teachers who have impacted me the most are those who have never stopped learning themselves. Dr. Pickett is one of these. She is not just intrigued with what the Bible says; she is passionately in love with the Author—and has been for a long time. That's what makes her teaching style so different from other biblical scholars. She doesn't hide the stirrings of her own heart as she writes. You'll feel her involvement with her subject is real.

Put yourself under Dr. Pickett's instruction. Challenge yourself to go through the paces. Enjoy the journey as your love for God deepens, as well as your understanding of all that He has said—and is still saying—to us through His Word.

—BRENDA J. DAVIS, EDITOR
SPIRITLED WOMAN

Introduction

Welcome to *How to Search the Scriptures,* a comprehensive study book to show you how to get the most from any Bible study you undertake. This course will provide you with a foundational understanding of how to search God's Word for the fresh revelation awaiting you. As you begin this study, take a look at your personal attitude about the Word of God. The following seven characteristics must be present in order for you to get the most from your study of God's Word:

   1. *Receive the Word of God with meekness.*

"Receive with meekness the engrafted word, which is able to save your souls" (James 1:21). Receive it as *servants* for it is the voice of the Master; receive it as *saints* to cleanse from all defilement; receive it as *subjects* for it is the command of the King; receive it as *soldiers* to be equipped for the warfare with evil; receive it as *saved ones* as the direction of grace; and receive it as *surrendered ones* as the rule for life.

2. *Let the Word of God dwell in you richly.*

"Let the word of Christ dwell in you richly in all wisdom" (Col. 3:16). Let it dwell in the *heart* as a preservative from evil; let it dwell in the *soul* as the propeller in service; let it dwell in the *mind* as the plan for direction; and let it dwell in the *affection* as the power for conflict.

3. *Keep the Word of God tenaciously.*

Christ could say of His disciples, "They have kept thy word" (John 17:6). We should keep it as a *treasure* securely, as our *teacher* for instruction, as a *tower* for protection, and as our *trust,* we should keep it faithfully and well.

4. *Continue in the Word of God untiringly.*

"If ye continue in my word, then ye are my disciples indeed" (John 8:31). Continuance in the Word is the *mark* of true discipleship, the *manifest evidence* that we are true followers of Christ.

5. *Live out the Word of God faithfully.*

"Ye are manifestly declared to be the epistle of Christ" (2 Cor. 3:3). The Christian is the world's Bible, a living object lesson. If we are not walking *Bibles,* then we are walking *libels.*

6. *Hold forth the Word of God boldly.*

"Holding forth the word of life..." (Phil. 2:16). As

the man holds the lighted torch above his head in the dark night to show himself and others the path on which to tread, so the Christian is to hold up the Word by his *life,* and its testimony with his *lips,* that others may be enlightened and benefited.

7. *Muse on the Word of God prayerfully.*

"He shall be like a tree planted by the rivers of water, that brought forth his fruit in his season" (Ps. 1:3). As the well-watered tree by the river's side grows and is fruitful, so the Christian who muses on and meditates in the truth of God is *prosperous* in life and *profitable* to others.

The companion SpiritLed Woman Bible Study Series contains three study guides, each twelve chapters long, designed to inspire women to study the Bible—alone or in groups. These booklets are ideal for group study and, at twelve chapters each, would work well as quarterly studies. The series includes study booklets on *Esther,* a study guide covering the historical importance of this brave woman's call "for such a time as this"; *Ruth,* a study guide relating the glorious love story of a woman called to the lineage of Christ; and *Deborah,* the fascinating historical account of one woman who obeyed the Spirit of God, leading a nation and becoming a deliverer for the people of God. With the addition of *How to Search the Scriptures*—this study you are about to begin—material is available for an entire year of Bible study.

Now, let's get started with our preparation study for all future Bible studies you will do.

All scripture is given by inspiration of God, and is profitable for doctrine, for reproof, for correction, for instruction in righteousness.

—2 TIMOTHY 3:16

Read

John 5:39; 10:35
1 Corinthians 2:13
1 Thessalonians 2:13
2 Timothy 3:14–17
Hebrews 1:1
2 Peter 1:19–21

1

The Bible Is God's Word

As the inspired Word of God, the Bible is
the supreme guide for faith and conduct.

Preliminary Consideration

Preview: The Old and New Testaments form a collection of sixty-six distinct books. These books were written in at least three languages by about forty different authors over a period of about sixteen hundred years. The authors lived under varying conditions in many civilizations and environments. Notwithstanding the many diversities connected with these authors, they all tell the one and only story that runs through all the Scripture. Each book is a literary whole, and at the same time each is a part of the larger whole, making its own distinctive contribution to the revelation of God.

The Bible is not a record of man's quest for God as he has climbed the ladder of culture and civilization through the centuries. Rather, the Bible is an unfolding of God's truth to man so man might find a path back to God and a basis for fellowship with

Him. Biblical Christianity is the revelation of God; it is not a man-made faith arrived at by the faulty guesses of men. The complete canon of Scripture—sixty-six books, no more, no less—is God's complete Word to us. The Bible alone is the Word of God.

Evangelicals insist on two things about the Bible— it is *divinely inspired* and has *absolute authority* in all matters of faith and practice.

Objective: This series of lessons deals with how to study the Bible. The first two lessons—"The Bible Is God's Word" and "How We Got the Bible"—are basic. The purpose of the first lesson is to establish an understanding of the inspiration and authority of the Bible.

The Inspiration of the Scriptures

> All scripture is given by inspiration of God, and is profitable for doctrine, for reproof, for correction, for instruction in righteousness: That the man of God may be perfect, thoroughly furnished unto all good works.
>
> —2 Timothy 3:16–17

The Bible is the most remarkable volume ever produced in five thousand years of writing by the human race. On this fact men must agree despite what they may think of the message and authority of the Book. The Bible takes preeminence over all other literature as to content, for its unity and structure are most remarkable. The Bible also takes preeminence in both circulation and influence.

What need be said about the influence of the Bible? History divides time by the advent of Jesus Christ.

Three of the most important dates on the calendars of all nations of the Americas and Europe are Christmas, Good Friday, and Easter—all centered around the life of Jesus on earth. Has another person's birth or death so influenced the world? More books are written about the person and work of Christ than all the next several dozen of the great men of history. Is there another who has so inspired the musician, the poet, and the artist to produce great works?

Little need be said about the circulation of the Scriptures. Shakespeare has been translated into forty-seven languages; Tolstoy, into forty-seven; *The Pilgrim's Progress* into one hundred; but the Bible, in whole or in part, has been translated into more than eleven hundred languages or dialects.

It is altogether reasonable to believe that God chose to give man a trustworthy account of His revelation of truth. The record of this revelation—the Bible—is infallibly inspired, given by God to man for his edification, guidance, and blessings. This is a foundational belief of Christianity. Christianity stands or falls with the truth or falsehood of the Bible.

If the Bible is only the work of men, we can never lean on it for spiritual support. If it is no more than a human work, it must be a mere compilation of the ideas of man about ethics and morality, interwoven with a record of Jewish history. But the Bible is more than the work of man; it is inspired of God.

Evangelicals in all parts of the world are united on the doctrine of the inspiration of the Holy Scriptures. However, there is an amazing divergence of opinion today about what is meant by inspiration. New ideas have appeared on this important tenet of the faith. But if there is one truth in which Christians must be firmly established, it is the doctrine of the inspiration of the Holy Scriptures. We must be clear as to the method of inspiration as well as to the fact of it.

Several theories of inspiration have been advanced down through the centuries, just as there have been various theories on such doctrines as the Atonement. It is important to note that the Bible has nothing to say on theories of either atonement or inspiration. But throughout the Bible there are repeated expressions to the effect that its words are words that God spoke through men.

Inspiration defined

Inspiration is a special act of the Holy Spirit by which He guided the writers of Scripture, making sure that their words were free from error and omission and that they conveyed the thoughts that the Holy Spirit desired.

The word *inspired* comes from the Latin word *inspirare* and means "inbreathed." The Greek word *theopneustos* combines *God* and *breath*. *Theos* means "God" and *pneuma* means "breath." These two words combine in the Bible to make *theopneustos,* which is translated "inspired by God."

The inspiration of the Bible means that its contents were communicated to the writers by the Holy Spirit. That which is inspired is God's Word—written by human hands, molded in some degree by human thought, and using human words. Under the influence of the Holy Spirit, the writers were prevented from writing anything but what God intended. God so controlled the writer that the words written were exact and correct.

God created man by breathing into him the breath

of life so that man became a "living soul." In similar manner God breathed into the writers of Holy Scripture so that each could record the inspired Word of God.

The Bible never states that the men who wrote were inspired; only their writings were inspired. The men were fallible; the Scripture they wrote is infallible. Moses lost his temper and killed a man, but that does not change the fact that the Holy Spirit kept him from error as he wrote the Pentateuch. A similar statement could be made about David. He sinned, and yet God used him to record portions of the infallible Word. We do not know how the Bible is free from error since inspiration came through imperfect men. In the same manner we may find it hard to explain how Christ could be truly free from sin if He was born of a woman whose life, however good, contained sin. We know what God did even though we do not know how He did it. God gave us the Living Word free from sin and the written Word free from error.

There is an analogy between the birth of Jesus and the authorship of the Bible. The Holy Spirit came upon Mary, and the "power of the Highest" overshadowed her so "that holy thing" born of her was "called the Son of God" (Luke 1:35). Jesus was a Jew, not a Latin, a Nordic, an Indian, or an African American. He was recognizable as a man, and no doubt He had the physical characteristics of the Jewish race. He was also divine, the Son of God. As the Holy Spirit came upon the virgin Mary so that she conceived the human Jesus in her womb, in similar manner the Holy Spirit overshadowed the mental faculties of the authors of Holy Writ and caused them to write the Bible. Their writings bear the stamp of human personality. The characteristics and vocabulary of the individuals are evident. But the writings are not contaminated with human failure, despite personality characteristics, any more than the physical Jewish characteristics of Jesus lessened His absolute deity.

What is meant by verbal inspiration?

By *verbal inspiration* we mean that every word in the original manuscripts was inspired by God. On the other hand we do not mean to say that the writers were mere secretaries who took dictation from the Almighty. The writers were not robots. Each Bible writer used only those words in his vocabulary that the Holy Spirit approved and prompted him to use.

In some cases this was direct dictation, as with Moses, who wrote exactly what God gave him. In other cases it was less direct but no less exact. Scripture passages supporting verbal inspiration include the following:

- 1 Thessalonians 2:13
- 2 Timothy 3:16
- 1 Corinthians 14:37; 2:7–13; 11:23
- Galatians 1:11–12, 16, 20
- Ephesians 3:1–10
- 1 Peter 1:10–11, 21
- 2 Peter 3:16

God used about forty men to write the sixty-six books. No two men were alike, but God used the vocabularies, styles, and personalities of each writer to record His exact revelation. In other words, human authorship was respected to the extent that the characteristics of the writers were preserved and their styles and vocabularies were employed without error. This involved a mysterious interaction between the Spirit of God and man.

What is meant by plenary inspiration?

By *plenary inspiration* we mean full inspiration of all Scripture as against partial inspiration. Verbal inspiration brings an accuracy that insures full inspiration for every portion of the Bible. To sum it up: The whole Bible is God's Word written by men.

Are there different kinds of inspiration?

Yes, there are different kinds of inspiration in these respects:

- There was divine guidance in the narration of facts and the selection of facts to be recorded in cases where the author related scenes and sayings that he had personally observed.

- There was inspiration resulting from the operation of the Holy Spirit on the human faculties on those occasions when the writing was not a narration of past events, a prediction of future events, or a declaration of the way of salvation. On the contrary, the writing was an expression of great moral and spiritual truth.

- There was divine guidance when a writer brought forth God's thoughts on great doctrines and moral issues or when he expressed

7

the inner thoughts of one when writing about Him. To illustrate—Matthew, when writing of the woman with the issue of blood, said, "For she said within herself" (Matt. 9:21). How could he know what she said within herself unless the Holy Spirit revealed it?

In every case inspiration is the direction of the Holy Spirit.

Inspiration declared

For the prophecy came not in old time by the will of man: but holy men of God spake as they were moved by the Holy Ghost.

—2 PETER 1:21

God, who at sundry times and in divers manners spake in time past unto the fathers by the prophets...

—HEBREWS 1:1

The historic doctrine of the verbal, plenary inspiration of the Bible is under grave attack today. However, the Christian must not base his defense of this vitally important doctrine upon the fact that it is historic. The doctrine must be defended because the Lord Jesus Christ and the Bible itself demand it.

We turn to the Bible for its witness and for the witness of none less than the Lord Jesus Christ Himself. He said, "What is written in the law?" (Luke 10:26). The apostle Paul in a similar vein said, "What saith the scripture?" (Rom. 4:3; Gal. 4:30).

Unquestionably the Scriptures teach their own inspiration. Over two thousand times the words "thus saith the Lord" or their equivalent are found in the Bible. There are thirteen hundred such passages in the books of the prophets alone.

When we turn to the Law we are struck by the recurring phrase "the Lord spake unto Moses, saying. . . " The entire Book of the Law develops under divine direction (Deut. 29:1; 31:16–19). Coming to the Book of Joshua we have reference to dual authorship of the Law (Josh. 1:1, 8; 23:6). Neither Israel nor Joshua regarded the Law as man's book. How then could it be called the Law of Moses? This is the proof of inspiration. The Word of the Lord was given through Moses as God spoke. The Law came by Moses, but it is the Law of God. Like its Author, it is perfect, without human stain, defect, or flaw.

No modern words about the Bible express greater warmth of gratitude and nobler veneration than the Book of Psalms. A few examples are Psalm 1:2; 9:7–11; and 119. David laid claim to verbal inspiration. "The spirit of the LORD spake by me, and his word was in my tongue" (2 Sam. 23:2).

The New Testament refers to the Old Testament as *the Scriptures* a total of fifty-nine times. There are 284 quotations of the Old Testament in the New, and they appear in seventeen books.

The testimony of Christ to the inspiration and authority of the Old Testament is beyond question. Not only did Christ meet each assault of Satan by quoting Scripture, but He also repeatedly referred to events in His life taking place as the fulfillment of Scripture. Never did the Jews accuse Him for His views concerning the Old Testament.

Paul states that all Scripture is God-breathed. He

declared that the gospel he preached came to him by revelation (Gal. 1:12).

Peter equates the authority of Paul's epistles with the Old Testament when he speaks of those who wrest Paul's writings "as they do also the other scriptures" (2 Pet. 3:16). Peter states that no prophecy came by the will of man, but came from God as man was "moved by the Holy Ghost" (2 Pet. 1:21).

The Authority of the Scriptures

Which things also we speak, not in the words which man's wisdom teacheth, but which the Holy Ghost teacheth; comparing spiritual things with spiritual.

—1 CORINTHIANS 2:13

Search the scriptures; for in them ye think ye have eternal life: and they are they which testify of me.

—JOHN 5:39

The scripture cannot be broken.

—JOHN 10:35

For this cause also thank we God without ceasing, because, when ye received the word of God which ye heard of us, ye received it not as the word of men, but as it is in truth, the word of God, which effectually worketh also in you that believe.

—1 THESSALONIANS 2:13

The Word of God is complete. It needs no additions

and tolerates no subtractions (Rev. 22:18–19). The Bible is an authoritative Book, having authority to control our actions and to give us an answer to our questions; it is the infallible, authoritative rule of faith and conduct.

The children sing, "Jesus loves me! this I know, for the Bible tells me so." The preacher cries out, "The Bible says . . . !" Why is such great store set by the Bible? Because it has authority. It is the Word of God! If the Bible is God's authoritative Word, then it is the expression of God's will. Ignorance of the Bible inevitably produces ignorance of God's will for our lives. If the Bible is the authoritative expression of God's will for our lives, it must have priority in our interest and study. Our chief concern must be to understand this Book. Since knowledge of the Bible will bring us to decision, the Bible will be either a minister of life or death to us. Our obedience will be the determining factor.

The words *inerrancy* and *infallibility* need explanation. *Inerrancy* means the state of being free from error. *Infallibility* means incapability of error.

The Word of God is infallible because God Himself is infallible. What the Bible says is to be received as the infallible Word of the infallible God. To believe in the inerrancy and infallibility of the Scriptures is to believe that they are of divine authorship and that God and His Word can be totally relied upon.

The infallibility of the Bible applies to the original manuscripts, not to translations and versions. Competent scholars have brought our English versions to a remarkable degree of perfection, however, and we can with confidence rest upon them as authoritative.

Is the Bible God's only final authority for us today?

11

Some question whether God's final authority is the Book or a church. The matter of spiritual authority is a most urgent issue. Some ask, "Did not the church give us the Bible? Has not the church been the guardian of the Bible? And must not the church take precedence over the Bible?" The answer is a resounding "No!" The church did not give us the Bible; God gave us the Bible.

The church has true authority only insofar as her principles and practices are in conformity with the Scriptures. God gave the Word through individuals, not through the church corporate nor through a church council. For the Christian, the Bible is the supreme court from which there is no appeal. Always it is God speaking. It is written! And the believer puts his trust in God's Word.

The difference between the Protestant and the Roman Catholic position is not a dispute about the inspiration and authority of the Word. Disagreement comes when the Romanist says that the church has the exclusive and final right to interpretation. This doctrine of the authority of the church was added at the Council of Trent in 1545.

The evangelical Christian finds himself in violent disagreement with both the liberal and the neo-orthodox. The liberal denies the inspiration of the Word; the neo-orthodox believes that those parts of the Bible that become significant to him as he reads them have authority. Some believe that the Bible is an imperfect instrument through which Christ, who is God's Word to man, is revealed. This implies that we cannot have confidence in the Bible. What then is perfect and what is imperfect? The answer comes strong and clear in an anonymous quotation:

"Scripture is from God! Scripture throughout is from God; Scripture throughout is entirely from God. The Bible is God speaking in man; it is God speaking by man; it is God speaking as man! It is God speaking for man, but always it is God speaking."

Illustrative and Practical

John Wesley has argued:

> I beg leave to give a short, clear, strong argument for the Divine inspiration of the Holy Scriptures. The Bible must be the invention of good men or angels, bad men or devils, or of God. It could not be the invention of good men or angels, for they neither would nor could make a book and tell lies all the time they were writing it, saying, "Thus saith the Lord," when it was their own invention. It could not be the invention of bad men or devils, for they could not make a book that commands all duty, forbids all sins, and condemns their own souls to Hell for all eternity. Therefore I draw the conclusion that the Bible must be given by Divine inspiration.[1]

One of the greatest leaders of the Church of England, Bishop Ryle of Liverpool, wrote, "Give me the difficulties, rather than the doubt. I accept the plenary, verbal theory of biblical inspiration with all its difficulties and humbly wait for their solution. But while I wait, I am standing on the rock. 'It is written.'"

---

1. *The Works of John Wesley* (London, England: Wesleyan Methodist Book Room, 1872. Reprinted Grand Rapids, MI: Baker Book House, 1979).

13

Hundreds of volumes that are gathering dust on library shelves insist that Moses could never have written the Pentateuch because writing had not been invented in his day. But tablets and inscriptions have been found that were written several hundred years before Moses and, ironically, were found in the very peninsula of Sinai where Moses led the people of God for forty years.

Scores of books have been written about the Gospel of John, which state that John was not the author, that it was written in the third century rather than in the first, and that it is nothing but a fable. But a mummy was found in Egypt whose funeral had taken place about A.D. 100—there was definite evidence to that effect. The body was encased in a shroud made of several layers of papyrus leaves. The outer layers were broad leaves; the inner layers were scraps glued together. Scholars at the Rylands Library in Manchester, England, carefully dissolved the glue that held the pieces of the mummy wrapping. Right in the middle was a large fragment from the Gospel of John—proof that the fourth Gospel existed as early as the last decade of the first century. John died about A.D. 100, so this page from his Gospel dates about the time of his death.

Quick Quiz

- What is meant by inspiration? Verbal inspiration? Plenary inspiration?

- Prove the inspiration of the Old Testament and of the New Testament.

- What is meant by authority? Inerrancy? Infallibility?

- Why do you believe the Bible to be the Word of God?

Key Verse *Thy testimonies have I taken as an heritage for ever.*
—PSALM 119:111

Read Psalm 12:6–7; 119:111
1 Peter 1:24–25

2

How We Got the Bible

*Over thirty centuries of diligence and
struggle have given us the English Bible—
a Book in our language that is the
accurate and authoritative Word of God.*

Preliminary Consideration

Preview: The Bible has a fascinating history. How
it has come down to us is a story of great adventure and marked devotion on the part of those
who, often at great cost, helped bring it to us. The
Scriptures were not written by mere chance, nor
has their preservation and transmission to us been
by chance. One of the most interesting and
thrilling chapters in church history is the story of
the transmission of the Bible.

Before the advent of the printing press, the
Bible was a scarce commodity. Laboriously copied
by hand in the monasteries, only a few copies
were available here and there. These copies were
so treasured that they were often fastened into
position with chains to prevent their being stolen.

Publicly denounced, the Bible lives on after the voices of its critics have been silenced in death. Translated in secret and red with the blood of those who died that it might live, the Bible is the world's greatest Book.

Many of God's saints have contributed to this great heritage by which we have received immeasurable blessing. Not all have been recorded in the annals of history—their names have perished, but their work lives on. This hall of fame would include such as Caedmon, the illiterate cowherd; the Venerable Bede; Alfred the King; Wycliffe, "the morning star of the Reformation"; and William Tyndale, whose labors produced the first printed edition of the Bible in his native tongue.

Objective: The English Bible is the greatest heritage of the English-speaking world. We owe so much to it. This lesson will relate in part the thrilling history of how we got our Bible.

Early Manuscripts

The earliest known examples of writing come to us from the land of Egypt and existed before Moses wrote the Pentateuch. History has been recorded on stone from earliest times. Clay and wooden tablets were used extensively in Egypt, Palestine, and Greece. Animal skin was in common usage for several hundred years during the writing of the Old Testament.

The most important writing material of the ancient world came from the papyrus plant, which grew in abundance along the Nile. Papyrus rolls (scrolls) were used until the first or second century after Christ. These rolls were about ten inches wide and thirty feet long. They were replaced by what is known as papyrus codex. In a codex the papyrus was bound together in sheets, like pages in a book, instead of being left in a lengthy roll.

Some one hundred fifty years before the birth of Christ, King Eumenes of Pergamum in Asia Minor perfected a process in the treatment of skins, resulting in what is known as vellum or parchment.

The Bible is a collection of sixty-six books written over a period of sixteen hundred years. These books were written on all kinds of materials. Possibly the Old Testament was recorded on leather or skins for the most part. Papyrus was in general use when the New Testament was written. Vellum displaced papyrus during the fourth century. The handmade copies of the New Testament for several centuries took the form of the vellum codex. The majority of New Testament manuscripts available to us today are on this beautiful and durable material.

The Bible was originally written in three languages—Hebrew, Aramaic, and Greek. Almost all of the Old Testament was written in Hebrew. Aramaic, the tongue of the common man in Palestine, appears in limited portions. The New Testament was written in Greek, the worldwide language of the day.

So far as is known, none of the original manuscripts are now in existence. There does exist, however, an abundance of good manuscript copies and ancient versions or translations. *Manuscripts* are copies of the original; *versions* are translations of the manuscripts. The Old Testament and New Testament manuscripts available to us today are ancient copies of the originals.

Until 1947 the earliest known Hebrew manuscript

of the Old Testament was one dating from the ninth century A.D. Then in 1947 two Arab goatherds happened upon an ancient cave high on the rugged cliffs at Qumran by the Dead Sea. They found several earthen vessels. In the vessels were eight leather scrolls protected by extensive wrappings of cloth.

Known as the Dead Sea Scrolls, they include all of the Old Testament except Esther; they date from the centuries just before and after the birth of Christ.

Obscurity veils the actual writing of the Bible. But the scribes who copied the manuscripts accepted the assumption of divine inspiration. They worked to the limit of their capacity with painstaking care for accuracy.

Scattered throughout libraries all over the world are about five thousand ancient New Testament manuscripts. In 1844 the German scholar von Tischendorf discovered in a monastery on Mount Sinai the famous Codex Sinaiticus, a magnificent parchment copy of the Greek Bible dating from the fourth Christian century. Another early manuscript is the Codex Vaticanus, which dates between A.D. 325 and 350 and became available near the turn of this century. Other manuscripts include the Alexandrian, the Codex Ephraem, the Codex Beza, and the Papyrus Bodmer II. The Sinaiticus, Vaticanus, and Alexandrian are manuscripts known as *uncials,* which means that they were written in large capital letters. There are also thousands of *minuscules,* which are manuscript portions written in running script.

The Canon of the Bible

What is meant by *the canon* of Scripture? The word

canon originally described an instrument made of reed or other material, used especially as a rod or ruler to make straight lines or accurate measurements. The word is used to distinguish the accepted books of the Bible from other books, such as those of the Apocrypha. It is important to keep in mind the fact that the canonization of a book does not mean that the Jews (in the case of the Old Testament) or the Christian church (in the case of the New) gave the book its authority. On the contrary, the authority of the book being established on other grounds caused the book to be recognized as properly belonging to the canon.

There is a difference between *canonicity* and *authority*. A book's canonicity depends upon its authority. A book has divine authority based on inspiration and then attains canonicity by its general acceptance as a product of God.

By the time of Jesus, the Old Testament canon had been established. Our Lord and His apostles made constant reference to "the Scripture." This implies that some writings were "Scripture" and others were not. Some writings were canonical, and others were not.

The Old Testament books, however, were not the only ones that the apostles, as Christ's authorized founders of the church, gave to the church as its all-sufficient rule of faith and practice. The gospel that the apostles preached was given by the Holy Spirit, and their writings were the depository of divine authority. Note these passages: 1 Peter 1:12; 1 Corinthians 2:13; 14:37; 1 Thessalonians 4:2; 2 Thessalonians 2:15; 3:14.

Writings such as the above were received as equal to the Scriptures. They were placed along with the

Old Testament books as a part of God's Word and were read as such in the meetings of the church—a practice required by the apostles. Note the following Scripture passages: 1 Thessalonians 5:27; Colossians 4:16; Revelation 1:3.

It is important to note that these books of the New Testament were given immediate place—under the seal of apostolic authority—in the canon. The apostle Peter, writing his second epistle in A.D. 66, speaks of the epistles of "our beloved brother Paul"— not in contrast with but as "other scriptures" (2 Pet. 3:16). In 1 Timothy 5:18, Paul quotes a Scripture passage from Deuteronomy (the Old Testament) in combination with one from Luke (the New): "For the scripture saith, Thou shalt not muzzle the ox that treadeth out the corn [Deut. 25:4]. And, The labourer is worthy of his reward [Luke 10:7]."

Let it be noted that the New Testament books were not gradually elevated to the place of inspiration and authority as God's Word. Evidence is conclusive to the effect that these books were accepted from the beginning as Holy Scripture. In other words, the early Christian church did not develop a canon of new books that tentatively might be considered as of equal authority with the Old Testament. Book after book was received from the apostles as equally "Scripture" with the Old Testament books. When the number was complete, they became the New Testament.

The New Testament was completed when the last authoritative book was given—the Revelation, written by John around A.D. 96. It is possible that some Christians and some of the churches did not have the completed canon until some time later, for copy work was slow, and a given epistle written to a given church may not have reached the general body of Christians until a later date.

Canonicity of a book was determined by the historical tradition of apostolic decision. It was not, however, apostolic authorship that, in the estimation of the churches, made a book a portion of the canon. It was imposition by the apostles of not only their own writings but of others as well that set the canon of the Bible. They, as divinely appointed founders of the church, imposed the books on the church as law. Determination of the authority of the various books was not by the authority or opinion of the church itself. By A.D. 691, at the second Trullan Council, the full New Testament as we know it today was completed.

Our English Bible

For centuries, the only Bibles available in Europe were the Latin translations. These copies were handwritten, for printing had not yet been invented. Being in Latin, they had no value to the majority of the people. With the spread of the gospel there came a desire in the hearts of the people to have the Bible in their own language.

Caedmon

The first attempts at putting portions of the Bible into early English occurred around A.D. 650 to 680. The earliest English translator on record was a cowherd or stableman in a monastery of Northern England by the name of Caedmon. He translated some of the stories from Genesis and other portions of the Scriptures into poetic verse.

Bede

Early in the eighth century the Gospel of John was translated into English by a much-loved scholar and literary man by the name of Bede, usually referred to as the Venerable Bede. Known as the "father of English history," Bede was the greatest teacher and scholar of his time. He wrote on a wide variety of subjects, but his religious works were his main interest. Before his death he had completed translating the Psalms and the Gospels.

Alfred and Aelfric

King Alfred the Great was the next translator, doing his work in the late years of the ninth century. Before the Norman Conquest in 1066, another scholar, Abbott Aelfric, had translated sizable portions of the Old Testament.

Chapter divisions

The division of the text into chapters was introduced by Stephen Langton, who later became archbishop of Canterbury. These divisions were made about A.D. 1250 in the Latin text.

Wycliffe

An honored name in the story of the English Bible is John Wycliffe, "the morning star of the Reformation." He and his associates became the first to give the English-speaking people the entire Scriptures in their own language (1380–82).

Invention of printing

The seventy-five-year span from 1450 to 1525 was momentous in European history. The mid-century witnessed the invention of printing. Few inventions, apart from writing itself, have had such far-reaching implications for human life and culture. Three men—Gutenberg, inventor of movable type; Schoeffer, his assistant; and Fust, a wealthy goldsmith who cast the first metal type—were important to the spread of the Scriptures.

Erasmus

Another important name is Erasmus. Possessing a brilliant mind and the excellent learning typical of the Renaissance, his was the scholarship that laid the foundation for impartial accuracy in the rendering of Scripture. Wycliffe had been forced to make his translation from the Latin. Erasmus edited a Greek New Testament in 1516 and became the pioneer in the field of New Testament scholarship.

Tyndale

It remained for William Tyndale, the English exile, to give us the first printed English New Testament. He published this first English translation of the New Testament from the original Greek in 1525. Tyndale also translated portions of the Old Testament from the original Hebrew, but he was martyred in 1536 before he was able to complete the task.

Coverdale's Bible and the Geneva Version

The first complete English Bible to be issued from the press was in 1535, the work of Miles Coverdale. The next important revision was known as the Geneva Version. Published in 1560, it was the Bible brought to America by the Pilgrims. It was the first to divide the text into verses.

Other sixteenth-century translations

Other translations included Matthew's Bible in 1537 and The Great Bible in 1539, so called because of its immense size—about nine by fifteen inches. It was also called the "Chained Bible" because it was chained to desks in churches. Every church had a copy in a convenient place per the command of the king. The Bishop's Bible—an attempt of the church to avoid doctrinal and controversial footnotes and aimed against Calvinistic influence—followed in 1568. The first Bible published in English by the Roman Catholic Church was the Rheims-Douay Bible (New Testament published in 1582, the Old Testament in two volumes in 1609 and 1610).

Authorized Version

This brings us to the masterpiece of English literature—the King James Version, which is the most popular and best-loved translation of the Bible in the world today. A committee of about fifty of the leading Greek and Hebrew scholars of the day began their task in 1607. In two years and nine months their work was ready for the press, and publishing was completed in 1611. The King James (or Authorized) Version is the last and best of the English revisions of the Reformation period. Many versions have appeared since 1611, but none have been able to dislodge the King James Version from its established position.

There are many factors that contribute to its supremacy. The men responsible for its production had a sure instinct for the sound of words as to style and prose rhythm. Harsh combinations of accents or sounds are distasteful to those who listen; by avoiding such harsh combinations, the King James

Version offers unsurpassed beauty for pulpit reading. The fact that it has survived the rivalries and challenges of over 370 years is tribute enough to this version, which stands at the pinnacle of literature.

American Standard Version

A desire for the full revision of the Authorized Version became widespread among Protestant scholars in the latter half of the nineteenth century. Many ancient manuscripts had been coming to light. Furthermore, many English words used in 1611 had changed in meaning, either entirely or in part.

As with the Authorized Version, work on the English Revised Version was done by the finest scholars of the day chosen from various denominations from both England and America. The New Testament was published in 1881, followed by the Old Testament in 1885. This was essentially an English revision, for the British committees prevailed when differences arose, mainly over British and American idioms and spelling. The result was the printing of the American Standard Version in 1901. Both eliminated many archaisms of the King James Version and made some improvements of textual readings, while preserving a faithful rendering of the original text.

Other nineteenth-century versions

Other translations, largely the work of individuals rather than of groups, include those by Alford (New Testament, 1869); Darby (New Testament, 1871; Old Testament, 1890); Young, of *Young's Analytical Concordance* fame (1862); Rotherham (1872, 1897–1902); and Newberry, before the turn of the century.

Current versions

Better-known current versions of this century are Weymouth (1903), Goodspeed (1923), Moffatt (final edition 1935), and Williams (1959).

The Revised Standard Version, completed in 1952, was launched with greater publicity than any other, yet it has not received great acclaim from the church world, particularly evangelicals. Probably few of the RSV committee held to a strict view of verbal inspiration. The principal complaint centers around the rendering of messianic passages of the Old Testament.

A translation that has gained wide acceptance is Phillips (1951). The Berkeley Version (1959) is more literal than Phillips' and quite conservative in nature.

Other efforts in interpretative translation include Wuest's Expanded Translation (1956–59) and the Amplified Bible (1958). These translations, faithful to the original and considered quite accurate, have their greatest value in private study. The Living Bible (1971) is a paraphrase in modern English.

An important addition to current versions was made by the publication in 1960 of the New American Standard Version. It is worded in contemporary English and at the same time is closer in meaning to the original languages than most other versions. The New English Bible (1961) is also a fresh translation, not a revision of earlier versions. Some of the most recent publications are the New International Version (1978), The New King James Version (1990), and The New Living Translation (1996).

No attempt has been made here to list all the versions and paraphrases that are available; only the better-known ones have been included. Most modern translations and amplifications are helpful if used properly. Wisdom is needed when choosing which Bible to read. Let it be said that the most forceful translations are those that are lived.

Illustrative and Practical

It was told of the Venerable Bede that all through the day before Ascension Day, A.D. 735, he had been dictating his translation of the Gospel of John. He said he did not want his boys (monks) to read a lie or to work to no purpose after he was gone. By evening only one chapter remained untranslated. The great scholar seemed very near death. All day, even though he was very weak and interrupted by farewells to brethren of the monastery, he had painfully translated on. By evening his sobbing scribe leaned over and whispered, "Master, there is just one sentence more." Bede instructed him to write quickly. The scribe wrote on and then said, "See, dear master, it is done now."

"Yes, you speak truly; it is finished now," Bede replied.

Then by his request they laid Bede down on the pavement of his cell, and he departed with the "Gloria" on his lips, to be with the dear Master whom he had so faithfully served during a long and devoted life.

Several hundred years ago the people of Bohemia were forbidden to possess or to read the Bible, according to an edict issued by the emperor of Austria, to which country Bohemia then belonged. However, many people refused to give up their Bibles, so soldiers were sent to search the houses and seize any Bible that might be found. When the people of any village heard that the soldiers were coming to their locality, they quickly hid their Bibles in some secret place. Although the houses were searched thoroughly, few Bibles were found.

One day the report came to a house that the soldiers were coming. A young girl there was kneading dough for bread. Quickly spreading out the dough, she placed the Bible in the center, doubled the dough over, put it into a big pan, and slipped it into the oven. When the soldiers arrived a few minutes later, they looked into every corner of the cottage but found no Bible. On opening the oven they saw only a large loaf of bread baking.

Years afterward the grandson of the heroine of this story emigrated to America, settling in Ohio. He brought with him the Bible that his grandmother had saved from the soldiers. It had been carefully kept as a relic of days that, fortunately, are no more.

Quick Quiz

- What was a papyrus roll? A codex? Vellum?

- Name the three original languages in which the Bible was written.

- Are the original manuscripts of the Bible available today? Explain.

- What is meant by the canon of Scripture?

- Name some of the early English translators and some more recent ones.

Key Verse

All scripture is given by inspiration of God, and is profitable for doctrine, for reproof, for correction, for instruction in righteousness.

—2 Timothy 3:16

Read

Proverbs 2:1–5
John 14:26; 16:13–15
2 Timothy 3:16

3

How to Study the Bible

The Bible deserves our devoted systematic study.

Preliminary Consideration

Preview: Regular and systematic reading of the Bible is essential for Christian growth. Spiritual success for both an individual and a church can come only through Bible study and meditation. A greater use and deeper understanding of the Word of God by believers is essential to a living, dynamic church. D. L. Moody said, "I never saw a useful Christian who was not a student of the Bible. If a man neglects his Bible, he may pray and ask God to use him in His work, but God cannot make much use of him, for there is not much for the Holy Spirit to work upon. We must have the Word itself, which is sharper than any two-edged sword."

The Bible is God's Book, given to us to tell us about God. We know there is a God because we see His creation—the sun, the moon, the stars, the mountains, the plains, the rivers, lakes, and oceans. All these and a thousand more are indications of the presence of a powerful Creator.

But we know little about God until we study the Bible. There we learn who God is, what He is, what He has done, what He is doing, and what He shall yet do. Man comes to the end of his search for truth when he sees the manifestation of God in the Person of the Lord Jesus Christ as revealed in God's written Word. From the Bible we learn that God is holy and that He hates our sins. But the Bible shows that God loves us so much that He gave His Son to save us from our sins.

The Bible tells us that we have sinned. It tells us that Jesus came into the world to save sinners, that He took our place at Calvary, that He arose from the dead, and that He is seated at the right hand of the Father, from whence He shall come to receive His own unto Himself.

These are the glorious truths related in fascinating detail in the Bible. Pray with the psalmist, "Open thou mine eyes, that I may behold wondrous things out of thy law" (Ps. 119:18). Prayerful study of the Bible will help us gain a full-length picture of God's provision and plan for us.

Many Christians do not get much joy and satisfaction—that extra something—from their Bible study. They have failed to learn how to make studying the Word a feeding process that results in spiritual nourishment and growth. Most Christians read a portion of Scripture each day as a devotional exercise. This is good; it is necessary and profitable. But too many believers follow the practice of merely reading Bible portions; they never read the Bible in any other way.

The Bible should be studied systematically. A

knowledge of the Bible, or of any one book of the Bible, comes by a definite plan of reading and studying. Reading Bible portions will feed the soul, but a Christian needs to grasp and understand the great truths and doctrines the Bible teaches.

Bible study must not be an end in itself. God has given us the Bible; it is to do something *in* us and *through* us.

Objective: Several lessons will be devoted to various methods of Bible study. This lesson is planned to outline some general principles for effective Bible study.

A Plan of Action

- Study daily.
- Study prayerfully.
- Study systematically.
- Study with enjoyment.

Preparation for Study

My son, if thou wilt receive my words, and hide my commandments with thee; so that thou incline thine ear unto wisdom, and apply thine heart to understanding; yea, if thou criest after knowledge, and liftest up thy voice for understanding; if thou seekest her as silver, and searchest for her as for hid treasures; then shalt thou understand the fear of the LORD, and find the knowledge of God.

—PROVERBS 2:1–5

Personal Bible study is a battle. One does not find too many people today who seek a quiet place with a book; the number is even fewer when it comes to Bible study. Distractions are manifold, and time runs short.

Christians need to evaluate how they spend their time. Unwise use of time is one of the greatest deterrents to Christian growth.

Bible study is the most effective tool of the Holy Spirit to bring the Christian into conformity to Christ. Understandably, Satan uses every device possible to keep us from the Word of God.

Rules to follow

1. *The Bible is God's Word.*

"My son, if thou wilt receive my words...." We must come to the Bible with the conviction that it is the Word of God through which God will surely speak to us. We do not need to prove the Bible first and then accept it; we accept it and then let it prove itself. If we doubt the authority of the Word, we cannot expect to receive anything from the Lord (James 1:6–7). We need to be like the Thessalonians and receive the Word of God as truth (1 Thess. 2:13). Many receive no benefit because they do not receive the Word with faith (Heb. 4:2).

2. *Obedience is required.*

"Hide my commandments with thee." The soul must be exercised by the Word. The Word must school us and change our lives. If we fail to translate the Word into daily practice, we will be spiritually anemic. Bible study brings renewed devotion to God. Even more, it produces discipline and determination resulting in the transformation of human nature. There is no better way to blind ourselves to Bible truth than to refuse to heed and obey it. The prophet Hosea said, "My people are destroyed for lack of knowledge: because thou hast rejected knowledge, I will also reject thee" (Hos. 4:6). We do not truly study the Word, or really know it, until we put it into practice in our lives. "Be ye doers of the word" (James 1:22).

3. *Listening is demanded.*

"Incline thine ear unto wisdom." The word *incline* means "to listen, to take heed." Luke 8:18 says, "Take heed therefore how ye hear." We need to incline our ears to the voice of the Holy Spirit. A first principle in Bible study is to learn to read intelligently. But more than that, we need the illumination of the Holy Spirit, for the Bible is a revelation of spiritual truth, and its understanding is dependent upon spiritual sensitivity. Consider every phrase, every word of Scripture. Let the Holy Spirit make it real to the listening ear.

4. *The heart must be yielded.*

"Apply thine heart to understanding." Heart-searching should precede Bible study. The Word has been likened in Scripture to seed. We must prepare the soil of our hearts to receive the Word so it will bear fruit. The psalmist prayed, "Search me, O God, and know my heart: try me, and know my thoughts: and see if there be any wicked way in me" (Ps. 139:23–24). Unless the heart is prepared, we will miss the truths of the Word. We must have a regenerated heart (John 3:3), a humble heart (Matt. 11:25), a willing heart (John 7:17), and a devoted heart (Ps.

37

119:67). We need to open our hearts to God and let Him prepare them to receive the truth of His Word.

5. *Prayer is necessary.*

"Yea, if thou criest after knowledge, and liftest up thy voice for understanding...." We cannot, by our wisdom, understand the Bible. In all our study we must carefully seek the help of the Holy Spirit. He alone can remove the veil from our minds. It is impossible to know the Bible without prayer. We need to join the psalmist in his prayer, "Open thou mine eyes, that I may behold wondrous things out of thy law" (Ps. 119:18). When we breathe this prayer in faith, we can expect the Lord to open our understanding as He did for two men on the Emmaus road after His resurrection: "Their eyes were opened, and they knew him...and they said...Did not our heart burn within us...while he opened to us the scriptures?" (Luke 24:31–32). And also for Lydia, the seller of purple: "And a certain woman named Lydia...whose heart the Lord opened" (Acts 16:14).

6. *Seek as for silver.*

"If thou seekest her as silver...." Silver is a standard of money. Men will do almost anything for money because money gives them so many of the things they want. The Bible states, "Money answereth all things" (Eccles. 10:19). Men work for the paycheck. But there is something of far greater worth than the silver of this world. David said, "The words of the LORD are pure words: as silver tried in a furnace of earth, purified seven times" (Ps. 12:6). As a man disciplines himself to hard toil to get a share of this world's goods, the Christian must prepare for the discipline of businesslike Bible study, coupled with businesslike prayer. It takes earnestness of purpose, concentration of effort, and determination of mind and heart.

7. *Search as for hidden treasure.*

"...searchest for her as for hid treasures." The word *searchest* is equivalent to dig. One translation (the Vulgate) reads "to dig out." The treasures of God's Word are to be found by the one who will give himself to diligently dig for them. We need to use the same untiring energy with which men dig for hidden treasure in our search for the riches of the Word. The perseverance of the seeker after material wealth often puts to shame the seeker after spiritual wealth. This matter of searching is important. Jesus said, "Search the scriptures" (John 5:39).

Results to expect
The serious seeker after spiritual wealth can expect the following results from study:

• Understanding

"Then shalt thou understand the fear of the LORD...." Our hearts will be filled with wonder and praise, and we will receive "the things of the Spirit of God" (1 Cor. 2:14).

• Knowledge

"...and find the knowledge of God." Purposeful

study will do more than merely give us the facts of the Bible; we will learn to know God. The divine Personality, infinite and unfathomable, will reveal Himself. We know the Living Word as we understand His revelation given to us in the written Word.

Provision for Study

> But the Comforter, which is the Holy Ghost, whom the Father will send in my name, he shall teach you all things, and bring all things to your remembrance, whatsoever I have said unto you.
> —JOHN 14:26

> Howbeit when he, the Spirit of truth, is come, he will guide you into all truth: for he shall not speak of himself; but whatsoever he shall hear, that shall he speak: and he will shew you things to come. He shall glorify me: for he shall receive of mine, and shall shew it unto you. All things that the Father hath are mine: therefore said I, that he shall take of mine, and shall shew it unto you.
> —JOHN 16:13–15

The Bible is God's message to us.

Every word has value and importance in the total revelation. The general theme of the Bible is redemption through the Lord Jesus Christ. Every part of the Bible is perfect because it is the Word of God. But the Old Testament by itself is incomplete, for it is anticipatory. It looks forward to the coming of the promised Redeemer. From beginning to end it is a book of promise, looking forward to something not yet fulfilled.

On the other hand, the New Testament speaks of the fulfillment of that expectation. The mighty sweep of God's purpose is given to us in Matthew 16:13–27. Here we have:

- The revelation of His person: "Thou art the Christ, the Son of the living God" (16:16).

- The revelation of His purpose: "Upon this rock I will build my church" (16:18).

- The revelation of His program: "He must go unto Jerusalem, and suffer many things of the elders and chief priests and scribes, and be killed, and be raised again the third day" (16:21). In the Gospel of Luke, God's purpose for this age is given in three steps: "It behoved [a strong word often translated 'must'] Christ to [a] suffer, and [b] to rise from the dead the third day: and [c] that repentance and remission of sins should be preached in his name among all nations, beginning at Jerusalem" (Luke 24:46–47).

- The revelation of the opposition to His program: "Be it far from thee, Lord: this shall not be unto thee" (Matt. 16:22).

- The revelation of the cost to be His follower: "If any man will come after me, let him deny himself, and take up his cross, and follow me" (16:24).

- The revelation of the culmination of His

purpose: "For the Son of man shall come in the glory of his Father with his angels; and then he shall reward every man according to his works" (16:27).

The Bible is clear in its central message.

There are depths of meaning that challenge the greatest minds and elude the grasp of the greatest thinkers, but generally the truths of the Scriptures are plain and clear. Satan wants to make us think that it is very difficult for the ordinary person to understand the Bible. Anyone who stands upon the Word need not be troubled with the fear of not being able to understand it, for understanding and enlightenment do not rest with us.

The Bible deals with matters that are divine, infinite, and eternal.

The Bible transcends man's understanding. But divine enablement comes to us through the Holy Spirit (John 14:26; 16:13–15; 1 Cor. 2:13–14). A yielded Christian, even though he may have a limited intellectual capacity and may lack formal education, can nevertheless make great progress in his understanding of the Bible, because he knows the Teacher and has daily fellowship with Him.

God has made provision for us to understand His Word by giving us the Holy Spirit. The Spirit who authored the Word is the divine Teacher who explains it. We must allow Him to guide us. Then it will be amazing how He will open our spiritual eyes.

The Word of God will not degenerate into a mere textbook of history or a manual on religion if we come to it always expecting an encounter with the

Lord. Study, illumined by the Holy Spirit, will bring us to worship. Meditation will bring us to praise, and praise will bring us to adoration. No better illustration can be found than the warmth of worship expressed by the psalmist as he dwelt on the wonders of the Word in Psalm 1, 19, and 119.

Principles of Study

All scripture is given by inspiration of God, and is profitable for doctrine, for reproof, for correction, for instruction in righteousness.

—2 TIMOTHY 3:16

God wants us to study the Bible. He has provided the Book and the Teacher. Through His servants we have an abundance of help in the form of Bible study books and study methods. If we have a desire to know the Word, a willingness to give time for that purpose, and a resolve to keep on despite obstacles, we will find the joy of learning and living in the Word. Come hungry to the Word, for the hungry are never disappointed (Matt. 5:6).

Bible study must be personal, practical, perpetual, and presented to others.

1. *Personal Bible study*

"O how I love thy law! it is my meditation all the day" (Ps. 119:97). Note the personal pronouns *I* and *my*. Bible study will be tedious until it becomes personal. Then it can be delightful, intensely interesting, thrilling, and profitable. In Bible study we must be participators rather than spectators.

2. *Practical Bible study*

Bible study requires a systematic approach. Do not stay only with those portions that have brought blessing or seem more inviting. If a less interesting passage falls into the plan, resist the inclination to turn aside. All scripture is inspired. *All* is God's Word. "Man shall not live by bread alone, but by every word that proceedeth out of the mouth of God" (Matt. 4:4). Aim to cover all the Bible. Approach the uninviting passage with a real spirit of study. Pray over it...meditate upon it...compare it with parallel passages...read what others have written about it. Watch it become real!

Actual study should involve reading the passage or the book over again and again. Read available translations. Make notes for later study. Keep a record of your observations just as they occur to you, whether they seem significant or not. Writing down your thoughts will serve to stimulate thinking and concentration. We discover how little we know when we try to write it down. Use a study Bible that can be marked. Marking your Bible will help to make your reading more concrete. Try underlining passages that are especially meaningful. Jot in the margins thoughts that the Spirit makes real.

Effective Bible study involves asking the following sequential questions:

- What does the passage say (content)? *Observation*
- What does it mean? *Interpretation*
- How does it apply to me? *Application*

As you seek to apply God's Word to your life, continue by asking: What does it say to me (personal application)? What does it say to me today (relevant personal application)? What am I going to do about it today (immediate personal action on the Word)?

It is necessary to *observe* carefully what the passage actually says before *interpreting* it, and then to *apply* the truths personally.

A simple, practical approach to study is suggested in 2 Timothy 3:16. Just as John 3:16 gives us the central verse of the Bible on how to become a Christian, 2 Timothy 3:16 gives us an important verse on how to grow as a Christian.

Any passage in the Bible—a verse, a chapter, a book—is God's Word and is profitable in four ways. Note them:

- *Doctrine:* The Bible presents a system of truth containing all the knowledge of God, man, and the universe essential to spiritual growth. Find the teaching of the passage.

- *Reproof:* Biblical reproof makes us feel keenly to what extent we have strayed from the divine standard.

- *Correction:* The Scripture is the plumb line by which we test the correctness of our thinking and the uprightness of our conduct. Some read the Bible to criticize and attempt to correct it. Blessing comes to those who read it for the purpose of allowing it to criticize and correct them.

- *Instruction in righteousness:* Biblical instruction applies the lessons learned in the passage to your personal life. As we compare our character and conduct with the precepts of the Scriptures, we are being practical about Bible study. Instruction is effective only to the extent that it is applied.

3. *Perpetual Bible study*

> These [the Bereans] were more noble than those in Thessalonica, in that they received the word with all readiness of mind, and searched the scriptures daily.
>
> —Acts 17:11

The Bereans were marked as noble people for two reasons: They welcomed the Word of God, and they searched the Scriptures daily.

Bible study has been compared to eating. If we expect to stay alive spiritually, we must keep feeding ourselves. We do not eat a week's supply of food for the natural body in a day; there must be a daily assimilation of food. Neither can we absorb enough Bible study in a day to last for a lengthy period of time. If spiritual strength is to be maintained, there must be constant feeding on the Word of God.

4. *Presented to others*

> And the things that thou hast heard of me among many witnesses, the same commit thou to faithful men, who shall be able to teach others also.
>
> —2 Timothy 2:2

What we learn in Bible study must be passed on to others. If not, our study can become dull and uninteresting. The constant outflow of water from a body of water keeps it fresh and free from the stagnant odors and scum of a dead body of water. We use what we have learned by sharing it with others. Sharing is an excellent way to make a truth real to us.

Illustrative and Practical

Other books we may read and criticize. To the Scriptures we must bow the entire soul, with all its faculties.

—E. N. KIRK

The Scriptures were written, not to make us astronomers, but to make us saints.

—MATTHEW HENRY

The Bible is the most thought-suggesting book in the world. No other deals with such grand themes.

—HERRICK JOHNSON

When you are reading a book in a dark room, and come to a difficult part, you take it to a window to get more light. So take your Bible to Christ.

—ROBERT MACCHEYNE

I am convinced that the Bible becomes even more beautiful the more one understands it; that is, the more one gets insight to see that every word, which we take generally and make special applications of it to our own wants, has had, in connection with certain circumstances, with certain relations of time and place, a particular, directly individual reference of its own.

—Goethe

Make it the first morning business of your life to understand some part of the Bible clearly, and make it your daily business to obey it in all that you do understand.

—John Ruskin

Nobody ever outgrows Scripture; the Book widens and deepens with the years.

—Charles H. Spurgeon

There is no book that will so repay time spent on its pages as will the Word of God.

—F. B. Meyer

Benefits of committing the Scriptures to memory

The benefits of memorizing scripture are many. Unquestionably the presence of the Word of God in the inner mind does tend, by God's grace, to sweeten and sanctify. And then in solitary moments, whether on the job, in private meditation, or lying awake at night, how beautiful it is to be able to listen to the voice of God talking out of one's memory by His Word unto the mind and heart. What a power to guide, to warn, and to cheer us. Many a moment that would be invaded by sin or darkened by sorrow is turned into purity and hope by a portion of Scripture—a verse, a passage, a psalm—said from memory. "Thy word have I hid [stored, lodged] in mine heart, that I might not sin against thee" (Ps. 119:11).

Quick Quiz

- How can one prepare for Bible study? Why is preparation important?

- What part does the Holy Spirit play in Bible study? Explain.

- Compare the importance of John 3:16 and 2 Timothy 3:16.

- Name some principles to follow in Bible study.

- Why should we present what we learn to others?

Read

1 Corinthians 2:13
2 Timothy 2:15
2 Timothy 3:15–17
Hebrews 4:12

4

How to Interpret the Bible

The Christian will find personal blessing and spiritual growth as he reads and understands the Bible.

Preliminary Consideration

Preview: All Bible-believing Christians agree that God has spoken in His Word. Of this we are certain. It follows naturally to ask what He has said. We do not profit if God has spoken but we do not know what He has said. This is the basic task of Bible interpretation, otherwise known as hermeneutics.

Ancient interpreters closed their eyes to the human elements of the Bible, all the while accepting it as a divine Book. They regarded the Bible as an archive of divine sayings. Mistakenly they tried to confirm their speculations and theories by it. The tragic result was that the Scriptures were taken from the common people. Among the Jews no one but a rabbi was considered capable of interpreting the Old Testament. Later, in the Christian centuries, many believed that only the church could properly interpret the Scriptures. During the Reformation the Scriptures were freed from the bondage of church tradition.

The Bible is a divine Book, but it is phrased in human language. The Bible is made up of words "which the Holy Ghost teacheth" (1 Cor. 2:13), and these words are understood only in their relation to each other. This is only one of many principles of Bible interpretation. To find agreement on interpretation, we must first agree on the principles of interpretation.

Objective: To define general rules of biblical interpretation.

A Plan of Action

- Accuracy
- Background
- Common sense

Hermeneutics and Interpretation

When two men, apparently led by the Holy Spirit, differ on the meaning of a Bible verse or passage, it leaves some people with a feeling of bewilderment. Most Christians can understand differences that arise between Bible believers and skeptics. By the science of apologetics, the scoffers are met on their own terms. On the other hand, when it is not a question of unbelief but rather one of interpretation, we look to the science of *hermeneutics,* which simply means "interpretation." The Greek word *diermeneuo,* translated "interpreted" in the New Testament, is essentially, if not exactly, the same from which the word *hermeneutics* is derived. Hermeneutics, then, is the science of interpretation.

Hermeneutics, or interpretation, is a true science and therefore has defined laws. To violate law is to invite error and failure. This is true whether the matter before us is solving a mathematical problem, a scientific theory, a Bible proposition, or even such a simple matter as baking a cake. The interpretation of the Bible is an exacting science. Knowledge of the Hebrew and Greek languages, of history, of geography, and of other general areas of knowledge can prove helpful. But one does not need to be a scholar to learn to interpret the Bible correctly. The Bible is not a closed book, shrouded in mystery. God meant it to be read, studied, and understood. This can be a fascinating experience for anyone.

The Bible is a book that requires reading, rereading, then another reading, and another and another, and rereading over and over again. And the message is never exhausted. The depth of its truths goes beyond the penetrating power of the greatest mind. Yet there are the great truths of the plan of salvation, which are plain and clear. The Christian is under obligation to read, to study, and to understand the Word of God.

We tend to interpret Scripture according to our preconceived notions. It is very easy to become biased. We are inclined to interpret the Bible in the way most favorable to what we want to believe or the way best suited to the manner in which we want to live. How then can we know what is right interpretation?

The principles of Bible interpretation can be summarized under three headings for the purpose of simplicity. They are the ABCs of Bible interpretation: accuracy, background, and common sense. Keep these principles in focus, for they are essential to guard against misinterpretation. Study the Bible with them in mind.

Accuracy

To understand properly, we must accurately identify all persons, places, events, and objects appearing in the passage. Further, all words should be accurately defined.

To illustrate, there are six Marys mentioned in the New Testament—the virgin Mary (Matt. 1:18); Mary, the wife of Cleophas (John 19:25); Mary Magdalene (Matt. 27:56); Mary of Bethany, sister of Martha and Lazarus (John 11:1); Mary, the mother of John Mark (Acts 12:12); and Mary, a Christian woman in Rome (Rom. 16:6). There are three men named James, ten different Simons, and four or five men named John. Peter was also called Simon and Cephas. Matthew also bore the name of Levi. Jacob was renamed Israel.

There are two Antiochs—one was the capital of Syria and a center of missionary activity, the place where disciples were first called Christians (Acts 11:19–26); the other, Antioch in Pisidia, was a city in Asia Minor (Acts 13:14–52; 14:19–21). Chinnereth, Gennesaret, and Tiberias are other names for the Sea of Galilee.

These few examples illustrate why we must accurately identify persons and places in the Bible. How can this be done? A Bible dictionary, the work of scholars, will help us, for it will list every person and place mentioned in the Bible.

We must also be sure to consider the true meaning of words. Bear in mind that the King James Version of the Bible was translated from the Hebrew and Greek in 1611.

The meaning of words is always changing. Some words of the older Bible versions are obsolete or have completely changed in meaning. For example, 2 Thessalonians 2:7 says, "For the mystery of iniquity doth already work: only he who now letteth will let, until he be taken out of the way." The word *let* meant "hinder" in 1611; now it means "permit, allow." Note another example: The word *conversation* as it appears in such passages as Philippians 1:27 and Hebrews 13:5 meant "manner of life, behavior" in 1611, whereas today it means "speech." For this reason modern translations are helpful. Some study Bibles give the modern translations in center column references or in notes.

The speakers and the writers of Scripture illustrated their messages and writings with expressions of contemporary interest. Common articles of their day were used. An understanding of manners and customs of that day brings understanding to passages such as "Neither do men put new wine into old bottles" (Matt. 9:17). One needs to study Bible history, Bible customs, and Bible geography to appreciate the significance and meaning in the illustrations.

Background

"A text without a context is a pretext," and therefore Scripture, whether a word, a verse, a passage, or even a book, must be seen in its proper relationships. Every verse in the Bible is set in its proper context or setting. Isolated passages taken out of their context are often misleading. The context generally holds the key to the meaning of the passage.

That "you can prove anything by the Bible" is true only if Bible words are lifted out of their proper setting. Psalm 14:1 states that "there is no God" if we take it out of its setting. But the whole verse reads, "The fool hath said in his heart, There is no God." Was Paul recommending a meatless diet when he said, "I will eat no flesh while the world standeth" (1 Cor. 8:13)? No, he was talking about abstaining from meat offered to idols and causing a brother to stumble.

From the Bible it can be shown that we should go and hang ourselves. We are told in Matthew 27:5 that Judas "went and hanged himself." In Luke 10:37 we read, "Then said Jesus...Go, and do thou likewise." Jesus said in John 13:27, "That thou doest, do quickly." All will agree that this is wresting Scripture completely out of its meaning to the extent of being ridiculous. But it illustrates the error of taking a collection of texts that we may lift at pleasure to use in any way we wish. This is never fair, whether the treatment is of a man's address or conversation or an author's book. The unfair practice of quoting people out of context is often a basis for misunderstanding and even character assassination. Think of how God's Word is dishonored by this practice.

We honor the Bible when we take it as it stands. We honor it when we interpret each verse and each word in the light of the total message. To illustrate, the Bible contains the words of Satan in passages such as Job 1:9–11 and 2:4–5. It also contains the words of the enemies of God and His people in passages such as Isaiah 36 where Rabshakeh counseled the people of Judah to surrender to Sennacherib, king of Assyria.

Scriptural promises and commands must be interpreted in the light of their context. God's command for Jeremiah not to marry is not an argument for celibacy (Jer. 16:1–4). It is interpreted by the context.

The social life of Judah was about to become disrupted and to cease in the land. Later the exiles in Babylon were urged to marry and raise children (Jer. 29:4–7). The command becomes meaningful in the light of the total picture.

We must bear in mind that chapter divisions and even verse divisions are imperfect, for they are the work of man. They are very helpful for identification purposes, but to avoid confusion we must consider them in the light of their context.

The meaningful passage describing the humiliation, suffering, and glorification of Christ in Isaiah 53 really has its beginning in verse 13 of chapter 52. The first verse of Colossians 4 could well belong to the third chapter. Each verse of Scripture should be studied in the light of the entire chapter, or better yet, in the light of the unit of particular truth. Each chapter should be treated in the light of the entire book.

Keep the following items in mind as background for a particular passage:

- *The speaker.* Who is speaking—God, an apostle, a prophet, a saint, a sinner, an angel, or Satan? What is the character of the speaker? If he is a man, what is his age, his experience, his background? The "lad" Isaac who trudged with his father Abraham into the land of Moriah to be offered as a sacrifice was a full-grown man. Many do not realize that Daniel was about ninety years old, not a young man, when he was thrown into the den of lions.

- *The addressee.* To whom are the words

addressed—God, man, saint, sinner, back-slider, individual, or a group?

- *The time.* When was it spoken? To illustrate, several of the prophets of the Old Testament were contemporaries. Amos and Hosea prophesied to the Northern Kingdom at the time Isaiah and Micah brought God's message to Judah. While Daniel witnessed to royalty in Babylon, Ezekiel sat with the captives by the river Chebar, and Jeremiah ministered to the remnant left in the ruins of Jerusalem.

- *The place.* Paul wrote to the Ephesians of "blessings in heavenly places" (1:3). To the Philippians he said, "For I have learned, in whatsoever state I am, therewith to be content" (4:11). These passages become particularly meaningful when we bear in mind that both letters were written from prison.

- *The main theme.* Bear in mind the occasion and the main subject of the passage. The principle will help us understand a passage such as, "Work out your own salvation with fear and trembling" (Phil. 2:12). The passage does not teach that salvation and heaven are earned by works. The theme of the chapter is Christian living, and the letter itself was addressed to those who were Christians (1:1).

Do not interpret a verse or a passage as an isolated piece of Scripture. Study it in its proper setting with all the passages related to it. This will solve many of the seeming contradictions over which some people struggle.

Common Sense

The Bible usually means exactly what it says. Wherever possible the Scripture should be interpreted literally. Attempting to find hidden, obscure meanings can lead to error.

A problem for interpreters is the confusion over what is literal and what is figurative. The Bible is filled with figures of speech such as metaphors and similes. The Bible is a piece of literature and should be used as such. We must recognize figures of speech when we see them. For example, we read, "Moab is my washpot; over Edom will I cast out my shoe" (Ps. 60:8). While this is God speaking, common sense tells us that this is figurative language, for it does not mean that God literally washes Himself or that He wears shoes.

Every language has its particular idioms. Metaphors, similes, and other figures of speech, while perplexing to others, are familiar in one's own language. Common examples include "ice water in his veins," "neat as a pin," "slick as glass."

The Bible employs many figures of speech. Being an Eastern book and written by Eastern men, it uses methods of expression and alludes to customs common to those areas of the world. Also the history and teachings of the Bible are from a culture of twenty centuries ago. An understanding of Oriental expressions will be most helpful to us.

The most commonly used figure of speech in the Bible is the metaphor. A *metaphor* is a figure of speech in which a word or a phrase, literally denoting one kind of object or idea, is used in place of another by way of suggesting a likeness or analogy between them. For example, "a ship plows the sea," or "he used a volley of oaths." Note a few of these fascinating figures of speech: "Ye are the salt of the earth" (Matt. 5:13); "I am the light of the world" (John 8:12); "I am the door" (John 10:9); "I am the bread of life" (John 6:35); "The LORD is my shepherd" (Ps. 23:1); "The name of the LORD is a strong tower" (Prov. 18:10).

Another figure of speech is the *simile,* which brings two objects into comparison to show their similarity. A few of these from daily usage will illustrate: "black as soot"; "white as snow"; "smooth as silk." Scriptural usages of the simile can be illustrated by Paul's portrayal of the Christian as a soldier in Ephesians 6:10–20. The Christian's activities and resources are presented in picturesque manner as the believer's life is compared to warfare. His armor, his foes, and his source of power are described.

On numerous occasions the Bible employs *hyperbole,* which is exaggeration for effect and is used legitimately as a symbolic term. A noted scriptural example is found in Matthew 7:3: "And why beholdest thou the mote that is in thy brother's eye, but considerest not the beam that is in thine own eye?"

Another category of the figures of speech used in the Scriptures includes types, parables, and allegories.

Types are found in the Old Testament with fulfillment in the New. A *type* can be described in the words of Scripture: "a shadow of...things to come" (Heb. 10:1). The type and the antitype do not agree in all things. Instead of identity there is similitude.

The Bible portrays truth by the use of parables. A

parable is a comparison, specifically a short fictitious narrative from which a moral or spiritual truth is drawn, such as the parables of Jesus.

An *allegory* is similar to a parable, only perhaps not capable of literal interpretation. A question then arises: How do we distinguish allegory from fact? The safest rule in understanding Scripture is to take it literally unless there is a clear indication, either from the context or by comparison with some other part of the Bible, that it is to be understood figuratively. Common sense tells us that when Jesus said, "I am the door," He did not mean He was a literal door.

Scripture must be compared with Scripture. The Bible presents all sides of truth, and all Scripture must be considered, for seldom does a single passage contain the entire teaching on a subject. Contradictions disappear as study continues. To illustrate, Paul states that salvation is by faith (Rom. 4:5), while James says, "By works a man is justified, and not by faith only" (James 2:24). Both are right. Faith alone saves, but it results in good works. Paul rightly states that salvation is by faith alone, and James warns against an alone faith. One condemns works without faith; the other, faith without works.

We arrive at proper interpretation by studying parallels of passages, of words, and of general teachings.

Finally, Bible interpretation should never be considered a purely mechanical or intellectual process; it must involve the Holy Spirit. Samuel Coleridge said, "The Bible without the Spirit is a sundial by moonlight." If we are to know the message of the Bible and to rightly divide it, we need the aid of the heavenly Interpreter, the Holy Spirit, who has promised to lead us into all truth.

Illustrative and Practical

The interpretation of a given verse will depend to a great extent upon who said it, to whom it was said, and the occasion upon which it was said. The following rather humorous illustration shows how this important rule is broken. The story is told of a pastor who disliked the way in which the ladies of his congregation piled their hair in large buns on the top of their heads. He preached a sermon on "Topknot Come Down." His text was taken from Matthew 24:17: "Let him which is on the housetop not come down to take any thing out of his house."

Augustine of old wrote the following on the difficulties of biblical interpretation: "Some of the expressions are so obscure as to shroud the meaning in the thickest darkness. And I do not doubt that all this was divinely arranged for the purpose of subduing pride by toil, and of preventing a feeling of satiety in the intellect which generally holds in small esteem what is discovered without difficulty.... Accordingly, the Holy Spirit has, with admirable wisdom and care for our welfare, so arranged the Holy Scriptures as by the plainer passages to satisfy our hunger, and by the more obscure to stimulate our appetite. For almost nothing is dug out of these obscure passages which may not be found set forth in the plainest language elsewhere."

Thoughts are conveyed by words. Every line of business has its own distinctive vocabulary. To the printer an "agate" is not a stone, a "dummy" is not dumb, and an "em" is not a letter. People today are more familiar with the vocabulary of automation and the space age than they are with the words of theology. A concordance and Bible dictionary will help us to understand and properly interpret ideas in the Bible expressed by theological words.

The ability to handle rightly the Word of Truth can be described in simple language. If we wish to unroll a ball of twine, we must look for the end of the string. If we start wrong, tangles are sure to result, but if we can find the end in the very center of the ball, how easily the twine comes out without any tangles until the entire ball is unwound.

Quick Quiz

- What is the meaning of hermeneutics?

- Name some of the laws of Bible interpretation.

- What is meant by context? What is its importance?

- Name some of the figures of speech used in the Bible.

- Cite instances of their usage.

When thou comest, bring with thee ... the books, but especially the parchments.

—2 TIMOTHY 4:13

2 Timothy 2:15

Hebrews 4:12

5

Tools for Bible Study

Bible study helps prepared by scholarly lovers of the Bible are important study aids.

Preliminary Consideration

Preview: The most important book to use in the study of the Bible is the Bible itself. Too many people read many books about the Bible but read the Bible itself very little. True Bible study must begin with the Book, for the Bible itself is primary.

All of us have had the problem of searching for an elusive verse. We remember it as being in Matthew—or perhaps Mark, or Luke—or was it in John? We can quote it verbatim, but we cannot locate it by chapter and verse.

Another problem is learning the meaning of a verse, obscured by the customs and languages of the people of Bible times. Really, is it easier "for a camel to go through the eye of a needle, than for a rich man to enter into the kingdom of God" (Matt. 19:24)?

Still another question—how tall was Goliath, "whose height was six cubits and a span" (1 Sam. 17:4)? How do we translate Bible measurements into present-day standards?

There are several basic reference books that can help in the problems that arise in our Bible study. Any serious, systematic study of the Bible will demand a certain minimum of study helps and a guided plan of approach.

Objective: For hundreds of years, accurate, detailed work has been done in developing helps for using and understanding the Bible. This chapter presents a list of Bible study tools that scholars have produced to help you study.

A Plan of Action

- The Bible itself
- Marginal references
- Concordance
- Bible dictionary and encyclopedia
- Bible atlas and history
- Topical textbook
- Commentary

The Bible Itself

A first requisite of Bible study is a study Bible. This should be one with print that can be read without difficulty. Choose one with paper suitable for marking.

Every student will want to use a King James Version. It is unsurpassed for beauty of expression in the English language. In addition, one could well have a copy of the American Standard Version.

Every student will find a good reference Bible to be an indispensable help. There are many different reference Bibles available. Here is a listing of some

of the better-known reference Bibles.
The Scofield Reference Bible: This is a much-used reference. The text is prominent in bold type with comments at the foot and numerous synopses on various subjects. Some of the notes are excellent, others are not perfect, and some are unacceptable to many. In places the comments are strongly Calvinistic. Unlike a number of other Bibles, it is not self-pronouncing. A looseleaf, wide-margin edition is available for those who wish to insert their own notes.

The Thompson Chain Reference Bible: This thorough and helpful work has a host of notes in the margin and an excellent section of "Condensed Encyclopedia" divided into more than four thousand topics. It also contains information on the canon and the principal English versions, an outlined analysis of each book, a number of maps, a concordance, and an index. It has a good harmony of the four Gospels and several excellent charts.

Dixon Analytical Edition: This Bible contains a dictionary, concordance, topical study, chronology outlines, and outstanding facts of each book, as well as information on the canon and various versions. References are footnoted below each verse, and textual revisions are bracketed in the verses.

Several other reference Bibles could be mentioned, such as the *New Oxford Reference Bible* and the *Holman Study Bible.*

Worrell's Translation of the New Testament: This New Testament with notes by the translator, A. S. Worrell, is published by Gospel Publishing House of Springfield, Missouri. It is footnoted with many helpful alternative renderings and explanatory notes.

The Englishman's Bible by Thomas Newberry has

been a blessing to many. It has marks and signs meant to give the ordinary English reader the full sense of the original Hebrew and Greek. The maps and charts of the tabernacle and temple, with explanatory notes, are valuable.

The Emphasized Bible: A New Translation by Joseph Bryant Rotherham, particularly sections containing the Old Testament notes, is useful as a study and reference book.

The Moffatt Bible translation has many brilliant insights, but the liberal theology of the author shows on occasion.

The New Testament in Modern Speech by Richard Weymouth is clear, simple, dignified, and sound from a doctrinal viewpoint.

Goodspeed's translation tends to be on the side of liberalism.

William's work is valuable, particularly in the translation of the Greek tenses.

Montgomery's work has been rated by some as one of the finer modern translations.

The New Testament in Modern English by J. B. Phillips, a paraphrase, is picturesque. Its low-keyed prose is almost casual. For example, the familiar "holy kiss" from the King James Version becomes "shake hands all around." (See 1 Corinthians 16:20.)

The New Testament: An Expanded Translation by Wuest is an interpretive translation, as is the Amplified Bible. Both are considered sound and helpful for study purposes.

Reading the same passage of scripture from different translations can shed light on the passage's true meaning as you ask the Holy Spirit to unveil the divine message it contains. But a word of caution should be observed. The majority of us cannot evaluate translations. Some translators have allowed their theological bias to enter into their translating work. For this reason it is wise to anchor our reading to the King James and the American Standard Versions, using other versions as supplements.

Marginal References

Although references in a Bible appear in various ways, the most common is the center reference column. Other methods are the side column reference, references under each verse, or at the bottom of the page.

The subject references lead the reader from the first clear mention of a truth to the last. In many reference Bibles the first and last references on a subject are in parentheses and are repeated each time. Thus the reader can follow the subject from beginning to end at whatever point he comes across it in his study.

As an example, in the Scofield Reference Bible the word *gospel* appears in Romans 1:16. Next to the word is a small *a*. The *a* in the center column gives the word and its other appearances in the chapter (verses 1, 9, 15). The next mention is in Romans 2:16; the first was in Genesis 12:1–3, and the last is in Revelation 14:6. The reference in Genesis 12:3 (small *e*) indicates the next reference in the chain is Isaiah 41:27. Thus an entire series of scriptural references on a given subject is tied together to inform the reader what the Bible has to say on it.

Referring again to Romans 1:16 in the Scofield Bible, we find another aid to study in the marginal reference column. By the word *salvation* is the numeral *1*. The numeral refers to the bottom of the page for a summary statement on the doctrine of salvation. This is typical of the footnotes to be found in this Bible.

Still another aid found in the reference column is an alternative rendering of a word or phrase. Let me illustrate from Acts 15:13–17. Verse 14 in the King James reads, "Simeon hath declared how God at the first did visit the Gentiles, to take out of them a people for his name." Turning again to the Scofield Bible, we find a literal rendering in the margin as follows: "God for the first time, i.e., in the house of Cornelius." The passage now becomes even more meaningful to Gentile Christians.

The margin also contains explanations of money, time, and weights in many Bibles. General statistical, geographical, and language information is also given by some publishers.

No particular publisher is recommended. It is recommended, however, that one learn to use the marginal references efficiently, for they can be of great assistance.

Concordance

One of the foremost tools for Bible study is the concordance. It provides immediate access to any verse of Scripture, even if one remembers only one word or a few words contained in it.

Three concordances are recognized leaders in the field: *Cruden's Unabridged Concordance, Young's Analytical Concordance to the Bible* (311,000 separate references to words and phrases in the Bible), and *Strong's Exhaustive Concordance.* The latter two are more comprehensive. Personal preferences vary as to which concordance is best.

The New Englishman's Greek Concordance and *The*

New Englishman's Hebrew Concordance, along with a Greek lexicon and Hebrew lexicon, can be of great study value for more advanced studies by Bible students.

Bible Dictionary and Encyclopedia

Another very important aid to Bible study is a dictionary of the Bible. Like any dictionary, it is an alphabetically arranged compilation of words and their definitions. A Bible dictionary contains words with biblical significance. Included are proper nouns—the names of persons and places—as well as common nouns with scriptural meanings.

Through use of a dictionary and an encyclopedia, the student can obtain a clearer understanding of difficult words and unfamiliar names of persons, places, and things. For example, the cubit, a biblical unit of measure, is found to be nearly eighteen inches. The word *penny* is discovered to be the translation of the Greek word *denarius,* which was the chief Roman silver coin, worth about fifteen to seventeen cents or the equivalent of a day's wages in Jesus' time. The common noun *stone* is treated with its particular biblical significance, with reference to the places where the word appears. The student can discover that the *hind* is a deer. The word *publican* is defined as the collector of Roman revenue. A dictionary will give detailed information regarding this class of Romans, hated among the Jews for their fraudulent exaction under the vicious Roman system of government.

The use of a Bible dictionary and Bible encyclopedia will enlighten the student when looking for the meaning of unfamiliar terms. Among the better-known works are *Davis Dictionary of the Bible, Unger's Concise Bible Dictionary, The New Bible Dictionary* by J. D. Douglas, *Smith's Bible Dictionary,* and the new *Pictorial Bible Dictionary* by Merrill C. Tenney.

Those who desire a more exhaustive treatment of subject matter may use *The International Standard Bible Encyclopedia* in five volumes and the *Dictionary of the Bible* by Sir William Smith in one volume.

Bible Atlas and History

Though of secondary importance to the basic aids already listed, a Bible atlas or geography, a book on biblical history, and a book on Bible manners and customs can make substantial contributions to the study of the Bible.

A Bible atlas helps the student visualize the setting of great events of Scripture. As a sourcebook of general information on Bible geography, geology, and archaeology, an atlas contains colored and outline maps and photographs. *Baker's Bible Atlas* is a good atlas for study purposes.

For example, the missionary journeys of Paul as recorded in the Book of Acts and the founding of the churches by the apostle, along with his later epistles to the churches, take on enriched meaning to the student who has a knowledge of the geography of the lands involved. The same could be said for the journeys of Jesus, Abraham, and other significant Bible personalities.

Bible manners and customs shed light on the understanding of the Bible as revealed in books such as *The Land and the Book* by Charles Page. A Bible handbook is a valuable tool to study. It may duplicate information in other types of books and could be a substitute to those who do not wish to invest in a number of books. *Halley's Bible Handbook,* for example, is a mine of general Bible information.

Topical Textbook

Students of the Bible use to good advantage those books that arrange subjects in topical fashion.

Nave's Topical Bible is a sort of concordance with texts in full, a digest of twenty thousand topics and subtopics, and one hundred thousand references to the Scriptures. Billy Graham has preferred this Bible for years, both for personal study and for platform ministry.

Commentary

A Bible commentary, as the name suggests, comments on the Bible passage by passage and verse by verse, interpreting its meaning. For hundreds of years Bible scholars and spiritual leaders have recorded the results of their studies, and much of this has been gathered in various commentaries.

Some commentaries are the work of a single author, while others are a compilation of the efforts of a number of men. Commentaries may range in size from one volume to well over fifty volumes to a set.

Since a commentary is written for the purpose of interpreting Scripture, care should be taken in selecting a set. Three of the better-known concise commentaries are *Matthew Henry's Commentary on the Whole Bible, New Commentary on the Whole Bible* by Jamieson, Fausset, and Brown, and *The Wycliffe Bible Commentary.*

My purpose here has been to initiate the sincere believer into a variety of study helps that will serve as effective tools for the serious student of the Word. A number of Bible study tools have been listed and specific titles have been mentioned. However, the list is very limited and does not necessarily give the best title in a given category. It may serve as a help to those who are beginning to develop a Bible study library.

Bibles with explanatory notes are convenient and prove helpful, but no Christian should merely read the notes in one Bible and think he has studied the Bible in its entirety. We cannot overemphasize the necessity of studying the Bible itself, studying independently of all notes and commentary.

Illustrative and Practical

A young preacher, sincere but ignorant of the change of meanings since the King James Version was translated in 1611, chose as a text "he maketh my feet like hinds' feet" (Ps. 18:33). He developed a message emphasizing the Christian's strength for service as God makes his feet like the hind feet of a horse, explaining that the strength of the hind feet of a horse enables it to pull a great load. Imagine the embarrassment felt for him by the many in his audience who were aware that the *hind* of the King James Version is literally a *deer.*

The labors of diligent men give us many interesting facts. Note these facts regarding Bible chapters and verses: The Old Testament has 929 chapters and 23,214 verses, an average of about twenty-five verses to a chapter. This compares to 260 chapters and 7,959 verses in the New Testament, an average of just over thirty verses per chapter. Psalm 117 has two verses; Psalm 119 has 176 verses, each one a declaration of the preciousness and power of the Word of God.

Quick Quiz

- Name some of the modern Bible translations. What are their advantages? Are there dangers in their usage? Explain.

- Of what value is a common dictionary or Bible dictionary for Bible study? Explain.

- How does one use a concordance? A Bible atlas? A commentary?

Search the scriptures; for in them ye think ye have eternal life: and they are they which testify of me.

—JOHN 5:39

Read

John 5:39
2 Timothy 2:15
Hebrews 4:12

6

Synthetic Method of Study

*Many books of the Bible remain dead let-
ters in the lives of Christians, mainly
because their readers have never caught
the large vision of truth contained in
them. We need the sense of the whole
before we seek to understand the parts.*

Preliminary Consideration

Preview: One of the best approaches to understanding the Bible as a whole is Bible synthesis.
Synthetic study simply means the study of the
Bible as a whole, each book of the Bible as a
whole, and each book as seen in its relation to the
other books. Synthesis is the opposite of analysis.
By analysis we take an object apart to examine its
parts; by synthesis we put it together and consider
it as a whole.

Many people believe the Bible is a Book one
can open anywhere and it will reveal its storehouse of truth. Such a practice will reveal some
truth to the casual reader, but it will not give him

the full message. To understand the Bible properly, one must grasp a comprehensive picture of its fundamental purpose.

The Bible requires study. Its hidden depths will not be revealed to the superficial reader. Jesus urged us to "search the scriptures" (John 5:39). The word *search* is a strong word indicating the use of energy, diligence, and application to the task. The prospector searches for treasure; the hunter searches for prey; the police search for the lawbreaker; the parent searches for the lost child. In like manner, we must employ a law of thoroughness in our searching of the Scriptures.

A proper study of the Bible should consist of a systematic study by books so as to gain a definite, comprehensive knowledge of the special contents of each.

Objective: As a preparation for a more exhaustive study, it is wise to take a forward glance over the entire contents of the book to get a survey of all the content. This lesson will attempt to outline a pattern of Bible synthesis and show it to be an ideal way to lay a solid foundation for further Bible study.

A Plan of Action

- Procedures in synthetic study
- Examples of synthetic study

Procedures in Synthetic Study

The Bible is the Word of God. Therefore, it is necessary for us to know the contents of the Book before we can know its interpretation. In other words, we must know what the Bible says before we can understand what it means. A first step will be to acquire knowledge of the factual content of the Scriptures. Next we will need to see the unity of the Bible, the relationship of one book to another and each to the whole. Further, we will need to see Christ and His redemption in all the Bible. Finally, we must make a personal application of the truths that we have learned to our own lives.

When you read the Bible for purposes of study, it is not enough to read one book and pass on to another. The same book must be read repeatedly—possibly half a dozen times—until the message grips you and begins to reveal its secrets to you. Many people read the Bible, even study it, but they do not get a grip on it. They fail to gain a working knowledge of its contents. To avoid this frustration, one could well adopt a plan of reading, rereading, and reading again a Bible book until its message permeates the spirit of that person. He will get a grip on the Book, or rather, the Book will get a grip on him.

Granted, a young Christian will struggle to develop a plan of maintaining interest in reading a book through at one sitting. He may find it difficult to grasp the teachings of the book in one reading, to note its construction, development, and purpose. It is important that one not lose interest before he begins. Shall a beginner attempt to study in another way? Shall he content himself by reading the Bible in tidbits and miss grasping the scope and sweep of the majestic argument as to God's plan and purpose? Or can a beginner find a way to read a text in the light of the context, and the context in the light of its relationship to the book, and the book in relation to the Bible as a whole?

Selection of the book to be studied is important. Begin by choosing one of the shorter and simpler books of the New Testament. It may be better to try to master a few books at first, such as Genesis, Exodus, Joshua, and Judges in the Old Testament, and the Gospels and some of the easier epistles in the New Testament. Almost every book was written because of some special need or circumstance; thus it has a particular background and serves a given purpose. For example, the Pentateuch lays a foundation of historical fact for the books that follow. In similar fashion the Book of Romans lays a foundation for the church and its doctrines. A grasp of Romans with its development of the great doctrine of justification by faith—the foundational truth of all Christian dogma— makes it possible for the believer to have a life of daily victory. Another choice of the book to be studied by a beginner might be 1 Thessalonians, 1 John, or 1 Peter.

After the book has been chosen, the student should begin by prayerfully reading it through, a task that usually takes less than thirty minutes. All the New Testament epistles except Romans, 1 and 2 Corinthians, and Hebrews can be read in less than half an hour. If a person keeps this in mind, he will not be so easily discouraged at the task. Give Bible reading a fair chance, and it will become fascinating as the Holy Spirit begins to illumine the Word. We must bear in mind that our reading should not be hurried. Many times our study will involve much time poring over a few verses or even just a word or two. But here we are discussing reading for the purpose of grasping the key information in a book.

Use the following guidelines to begin your synthetic study of the Bible:

- Read the book of your choice.

- Read it as a total unit, without observing its divisions into chapters and verses.

- Read it repeatedly until you have a grasp of its outline.

- Read it independently at first, without the aid of any commentary or other Bible help.

- Read it prayerfully, relying upon the Holy Spirit who wrote it to enlighten its pages to your understanding.

The first readings of a book may not leave much impression. But faithful, prayerful, and systematic reading will not be fruitless. Soon details will begin to take shape in your mind. By persistent reading of a book, you will become familiar with it and will be able to handle it freely.

There are certain things to look for when reading a book. Someone expressed it effectively as follows:

> The author, scope, occasion, theme, time, place, and next the form: these seven let him attend that reads the text.

To understand a book it is important to learn who the author is and what can be known about him. For instance, a study of Paul, Peter, and John will reveal interesting facts about each. They could be called *apostles of the three cardinal graces.* Paul might be called the apostle of faith; Peter, the apostle of hope;

and John, the apostle of love. Note how their lives, their actions, and their writings emphasize these lines of truth.

The first reading of a book should be done steadily, not so quickly that one cannot properly understand, but let it be done without stopping to deal with any questions that arise. That can be done later. On a second or third reading certain things will become evident. It may be certain expressions, often repeated by the writer, that come to the reader's attention. For instance, the Gospel of Mark has a characteristic expression or two. The writer often uses the terms *straightway* and *immediately*. These words are keys to understanding. These two characteristic expressions are the words of a servant. Mark pictures Jesus as the Servant. The servant character of the Son of God is pictured everywhere. There is the key word *better* in the Book of Hebrews that is used to portray the contrast of the good things of Judaism and the better things of Christ. As a further illustration, trace the usage of the word *precious* by Peter in his two epistles.

Use a notebook to jot down the things that begin to become evident. As you continue to read, an understanding of what the book is about will begin to form in your mind.

In pursuing the synthetic method of Bible study, we try first to discover the scope of a particular book. We will want to see the ground it covers and get a bird's-eye view of the subject it deals with so we can discover the purpose for which it was written. Every book has a theme and a purpose. The discovery of a key word or phrase can be a clue to understanding the purpose of the book. For instance, the key phrase of Romans is *the righteousness of God.* Paul wrote this epistle for the purpose of making it plain to all that righteousness comes by God and from Him alone. The church must ever guard against the error of salvation by works.

Examples of Synthetic Study

After repeated readings of any book of the Bible, one begins to see the aim of the author, and the contents begin to form an orderly pattern in the mind. Let us take a look at some examples.

The Book of Genesis
Genesis is *the book of beginnings.* It records the beginning of the heavens and the earth, of plant, animal, and human life, and of human relationships and institutions.

Genesis records the history of Creation, the Fall of man, the flood, and the beginning of nations. It relates the biographies of Abraham, Isaac, Jacob, and Joseph.

The purpose of Genesis is to reveal God's will and purpose in Creation and Redemption from the time of Creation to the time of the beginning of His chosen nation, Israel.

The key word of Genesis is *generations,* which means "descendants, issue, posterity, that is, persons and things created or produced." The word occurs in the following instances: "generations of the heavens and of the earth" (2:4); "generations of Adam" (5:1); "generations of Noah" (6:9); "generations of the sons of Noah" (10:1); "generations of Shem" (11:10); "generations of Terah" (11:27); "generations of Ishmael, Abraham's son" (25:12); "generations of Isaac" (25:19); "generations of

Esau" (36:1); and "generations of Jacob" (37:2).

Certain facts stand in bold relief as we read Genesis. Note the following as they bring a sweeping picture of the book.

The first great fact is *Creation*. This is covered in the first two chapters. Genesis 1 outlines the events of the six days of creation—1) light; 2) firmament; 3) dry land, sea, and plant life; 4) sun, moon, and stars; 5) fish and fowl; 6) animals and man. The second chapter describes in greater detail the creation of man. (This return to describe a matter in more detail is a pattern that the Holy Spirit uses again and again in the Bible. It is generally referred to as "the Law of Recurrence.")

The second outstanding fact of Genesis is the *Fall*, the beginning of sin among men. Chapters 3 and 4 deal with this matter. Again one finds details that form an outline—the temptation of the serpent (3:1–5); the fall of Eve and Adam (3:6–7); the seeking God (3:8–13); the curse (3:14–20); the provision of covering (3:21); the expulsion from Eden (3:22–24). Chapter 4 records the first murder and the first civilization.

The third great fact is the *flood,* which is dealt with in chapters 5 through 9. Lesser details include the genealogy of Noah (chapter 5), the building of the ark (chapter 6), the flood (chapter 7), the return to the land (chapter 8), and the covenant with Noah (chapter 9).

The fourth great fact is *the beginning of nations* (chapters 10 and 11). This was occasioned by the confusion of tongues as a result of God's judgment at Babel.

The fifth great fact is *the call of Abraham*. The Holy Spirit uses chapters 12 to 25 to record events relating to the life of Abraham. Again there is the list of lesser details, from the time of his call (12:1–3) to his death (25:7–10). Man had turned away from God. The Lord chose Abraham to father a chosen nation, Israel. From him came the lineage that provided the promised Redeemer. Of special note are the types of Christ and His redemption in these chapters: Melchizedek (14:18–20; cf. Heb. 7; Ps. 110) and the substitute ram offered in Isaac's stead (22:13–14). The apostle Paul used Abraham as an illustration of justifying faith in Romans 4.

The *biography of Isaac* follows next (chapters 21–28). Isaac is noteworthy as a type of Christ—a type in his birth, which was both supernatural and predicted; a type in his sacrifice when offered by his father as an only son. His return from the place of sacrifice was a type of Christ's resurrection. The incidents surrounding his marriage to Rebekah offer several beautiful pictures of Christ and His bride.

The seventh major fact of Genesis is *the history of Jacob* (chapters 25–36). Major lessons to be learned from the life of Jacob are: 1) the grace of God as manifested on behalf of Jacob; 2) the illustration of prevailing prayer at Peniel; 3) God's estimate of faith, for Jacob received the Lord's blessing because of his appreciation of spiritual things; 4) when Laban cheated Jacob it bore out the fact that "whatsoever a man soweth, that shall he also reap."

The last biography is that of *Joseph,* to whom God saw fit to devote the greater part of fourteen chapters of Genesis. As with Isaac, there are many types of Christ in the life of Joseph: 1) his father's love for him (37:3; cf. John 5:20); 2) the hatred of his brethren (37:8–27; cf. Matt. 27:1–2, 22–23); 3) his temptation (39:7–20; cf. Matt. 4:1–11); 4) his promotion by

Pharaoh (41:40–44; cf. Mark 16:19); 5) his marriage to a Gentile bride during his rejection by his brethren (41:45; cf. Acts 15:14); 6) his revelation of himself to his brethren (45:3; cf. Zech. 12:10).

A brief recap will indicate the following outline of Genesis, which will help one to think through the book.

Primeval	*Patriarchal*
(Chapters 1–11)	(Chapters 12–50)
Creation (chapters 1–2)	Abraham (chapters 12–25)
Fall (chapters 3–4)	Isaac (chapters 21–28)
Flood (chapters 5–9)	Jacob (chapters 25–36)
Nations (chapters 10–11)	Joseph (chapters 37–50)

The Gospel of Matthew

The writers of the four Gospels all present Jesus, but each present Him from a different viewpoint. None attempt a complete biography. They select incidents and discourses to emphasize the particular message to meet the needs of the people to whom they wrote. All wrote to all mankind, but each wrote primarily for a particular group.

Matthew intended his message primarily for the Jews. Mark wrote to a military people, the Romans. Luke presents Jesus as the perfect divine Man, addressing himself particularly to the Greeks, whose ideal was the perfect man—perfect morally, spiritually, and physically. John's testimony is given to prove that Jesus is the Christ, the Son of the living God, and is addressed to the church in general.

Matthew presents Jesus to us as He is revealed in His words. His Gospel shows Christ to us through the Lord's speech, words, sayings, discourses, and doctrines. As Matthew writes, he refers to and unfolds the significance of the past.

The purpose and the scope of the book are indicated in the first verse: "The book of the generation of Jesus Christ, the son of David, the son of Abraham." As the Son of David, Jesus is shown as *King;* as the son of Abraham, He is *obedient unto death.* The word *kingdom* occurs fifty-six times, *kingdom of heaven* thirty-two times, and *son of David* nine times.

The key idea is the word *fulfilled* or the phrase *that it might be fulfilled.* Matthew makes at least sixty references to the Old Testament writings as fulfilled in Christ.

Repeated readings of the Gospel of Matthew will bring truths to a person as stated above. These facts will help the reader get a bird's-eye view of the whole book. An outline of the book will develop in the mind. George Henderson, in *The Wonderful Word,** has given the following simple outline of Matthew's Gospel.

1. The Person of the King (1–4:16)
   (a) His relation to earth: true but sinless man (chapters 1–2)
   (b) His relation to heaven: beloved of the Father (chapter 3)
   (c) His relation to hell: conqueror of the devil (chapter 4)

2. The Preaching of the King (4:17–16:20)

From that time Jesus began to preach.
                                            —Matthew 4:17

---

*Henderson, George, *The Wonderful Word* (UK-Scotland: B. McCall Barbour, 1979).

3. The Passion of the King (16:21–28)

> From that time forth began Jesus to shew unto
> his disciples, how that he must...suffer...and
> be killed....
>
> —MATTHEW 16:21

Bible synthesis is meant to be more than an intellectual feast. If we approach the Bible with a
proper attitude of prayer, we can expect to find great
truths to enrich us spiritually, mentally, and physically.

Illustrative and Practical

Two ministers attended a conference. The one admired
the other for his calmness, cheerfulness, and poise.
One day he asked him the secret of his Christlike-
ness. "I confess I have not this control over my temper,
this cheerfulness, and this poise under provocation,"
he said. "How did it become yours? Is it natural or
acquired, and how?"

"It is not my nature to be patient and unruffled," said
his friend. "God delivered me from impatience and ill
temper through reading the Epistle to the Ephesians."

His friend was perplexed. "I also have read that
epistle often, and have preached on it scores of times,"
he said. "Did the change come because you read it in
a special way?"

"Well, yes," was the reply. "I read Ephesians twenty-
one times in twenty-one days."

"And what happened?" asked his friend.

"In that three weeks, as the thread of that great
letter emerged more and more clearly to me, God

lifted me into the heavenlies where irritability and impatience are impossible."

It has been told that D. L. Moody hoed his father's cornfield when he was a boy. He did such a poor job of it that he had to lay a stick at the place he left off at the end of the day if he was to find the place to begin the next day. Some people read and study their Bibles in this same way.

What should we do with the Bible? Answers one anonymous writer:

> Know it in the head,
> Stow it in the heart,
> Show it in the life,
> Sow it in the world;
> Read it to be wise,
> Believe it to be safe,
> Practice it to be holy.

Synthetic Bible study can be likened to an explorer climbing a high mountain to get a bird's-eye view of the whole area before exploring it in detail.

> Read it—
> Slowly,
> Frequently,
> Prayerfully,
> Reverently,
> Dig it up,
> Write it down,
> Pray it in,
> Live it out,
> Pass it on.

Quick Quiz

- What is meant by Bible synthesis?

- Name the rules to follow in synthetic study.

- What are the advantages of this type of Bible study?

- Give a brief outline of the Book of Genesis. What is the purpose and the key word of the book?

- Do the same for the Gospel of Matthew.

Blessed be the God and Father of our Lord Jesus Christ, who hath blessed us with all spiritual blessings in heavenly places in Christ.
—EPHESIANS 1:3

Ephesians 1:3, 14

7

Inductive Method of Study

The more we read and study the inexhaustible riches of Bible truth, the more convinced we are that no better investment of time can be made.

Preliminary Consideration

Preview: The Bible is unique among all the books of literature. It is a library, made up of sixty-six books, long and short, authored by about forty men over a period of about sixteen hundred years. Despite its diverse authorship over this long period of time, it has a oneness or unity of message. This overall unity indicates the purposeful design of the Almighty, for the Word of God is like a skillfully constructed building.

Bible study is a lifetime occupation. It is a task that is always unfinished. The previous chapter dealt with the synthetic study of the Bible; this chapter will deal with a more intensive approach to Bible study.

In the inductive, or direct, method of Bible study

we carefully examine a particular passage of the Word of God for the purpose of understanding its content, meaning, and application. This involves observation, interpretation, and application, or to put it another way, the student must discover what the author intended to say, recognize what he meant, and then receive his message by submissiveness and obedience of spirit. We observe, then conclude. This requires analysis, which tells us what a passage actually had to say. At first we notice only that which is obvious, but continued study will train us to discover deeper truths.

Bible analysis places emphasis upon the thread of truth. This thread can be found in a book, a chapter, a paragraph, even a verse. Finding the thread points up the essential unity of the Bible.

Objective: To teach the Bible student to dig into the Word, learning *how* to think rather than *what* to think.

A Plan of Action

- Procedure in inductive study
- Example of inductive study

Procedure in Inductive Study

Use the following steps of inductive study as you search the Scriptures for a deeper revelation of the mind of God.

Observation: What does the passage say?

In literature, form or structure of the text is important—it is the key to be used in unlocking the contents. Any literary work is constructed around one main structural framework. Study reveals that the basic structure is made up of smaller units of composition. These are seen to be related to each other and to the whole.

The Bible is great literature—and more. The application of the basic principle of literature is important in our study of the Bible. The Holy Spirit moved upon men of old to write words in the structural framework of this great Book that are meaningful in contributing to the whole. In other words, the writers did not record unrelated and aimless words. All that was said was inspired of God and was written with purpose.

The Holy Spirit directed each writer of Scripture to record only those things that needed to be said on a given subject; seldom, if ever, was everything included that could be said on a matter, whether it was a discourse, a biography, or a historical record. The Bible is not and does not claim to be a record of history, a text on science, or a code of ethics. Instead the authors were inspired to select those things that would accomplish the purpose of their books. The material selected was arranged to suit that purpose. For example, review the comments in the previous chapter regarding the choices of events and discourses chosen by the writers of the four Gospels, and note the expressions peculiar to each writer as he develops the theme and purpose of his book.

To analyze a given passage properly and understand the intent and meaning of the author, we must give attention to the content and form. All that God authors has order, form, and purpose. We must discipline ourselves to see this picture in the Scripture; it is not enough to study some parts and bypass others.

We must let the Bible speak for itself. In our quest to know God's truth as revealed in the Scriptures, we ask, "What does God say? How does He say it?"

Every passage of Scripture contains a principal truth. In addition to the primary meaning, there often is a less obvious truth. A certain truth in a given passage may be very evident, while on the other hand, there could be a less apparent gem to be dug out by the observing student. The Bible student has the task of ascertaining what the Holy Spirit intended to say.

How do we determine the true meaning of a passage? What is literal? What is symbolic? Before we can correctly interpret a portion of Scripture, we must correctly observe these features.

Diligent application of five steps is required to observe Scripture properly: 1) read; 2) record; 3) search; 4) relate; 5) recall.

Bible study begins and ends with *reading*. Paul writes, "Give attendance to reading" (1 Tim. 4:13). The diligent Bible student will make notes as he pursues his study. He will want to record his observations and be able to recall through meditation that which the Holy Spirit has made real to him. Someone has said that a pencil is the third eye for seeing scriptural truth. The other two are the eye of the Holy Spirit and the physical eye. To study with pencil and notebook at hand cultivates the powers of observation, orderly thought, and memory.

The Holy Spirit has caused Scripture to be *recorded* in a manner to challenge the student. The secrets of the Word are as "silver" and "hid treasures" that are to be sought after (Prov. 2:4). Sanctified effort is needed for this *searching* of the Word. Jesus commanded us to "search the scriptures" (John 5:39).

A next step in finding the meaning of a passage is to *relate* it to other passages. The Bible does not contradict itself. Truth is many-sided. Both Paul and James draw their respective arguments regarding faith and works from the same Old Testament patriarch—Abraham. Paul writes of obedience in faith, and James writes of obedience in action. They deal with complementary aspects of one truth. The better things of Christ as recorded in the epistle to the Hebrews take on enriched meaning as we become acquainted with the tabernacle of Moses and the Old Testament offerings.

Thus far these steps of observation have required concentration and effort. The next, *recall,* requires something else—meditation. The word *meditate* is from a Greek word meaning "to attend." To meditate is to give attention, to ponder prayerfully. This is what the Book of Proverbs admonishes us to do: "Incline thine ear...apply thine heart" (Prov. 2:2).

Exploring God's Word is a stimulating experience, for it leads to the thrill of discovery. Not only is the student edified, but he becomes inspired to share the truths learned. This leads to "great conversations" as the treasures are shared with others. Obscure passages become meaningful through the illumination of the Holy Spirit.

The record we keep of all our observations is important. Whether or not the items that occur to us seem important or not, let us record them. The noting of small items, seemingly insignificant at the time, may take on prominence as we begin to sift our observations.

As you dig deeper into the Word, note the following: 1) points; 2) problems (What does this passage say that I don't understand?); 3) parallels (What similar truths are found elsewhere in the Bible?); 4) precepts to obey; 5) promises to claim; 6) perils to avoid.

G. Campbell Morgan outlined four rules for this kind of study. He said, "Read and gain an impression. Think and gain an outline. Meditate and gain an analysis. Sweat and gain an understanding."

Interpretation: What does the passage mean?

To know what the author says puts us well on the way to understanding what he means. Correct observation is necessary for correct interpretation.

A passage may have only one interpretation but several applications. Paul wrote, "These things were our examples...they are written for our admonition" (1 Cor. 10:6, 11). In this instance Paul makes application of the things that happened to the children of Israel during their wanderings in the wilderness. Many Bible passages could be cited as having but one meaning, but their moral principles may be used for many applications.

One should determine the meaning of a passage, not verify his prejudices or traditions. Martin Luther advised that effort should be made to find the meaning of a passage, not import one into it. It is wrong to use verses as hooks upon which to hang doctrinal beliefs. For example, the mention of the word *water* in John 3:5 does not give license to teach baptismal regeneration. Passing references are not to be used for establishing doctrine.

Not all Scripture is easily understood. We may even grasp a Bible truth and yet never understand all of the implications of that truth. One of the enriching experiences of Bible study is the constant discovery of fresh truths. We will never exhaust the great riches of Bible content this side of eternity. When the writer finds a passage to be totally beyond his comprehension, he recognizes that "the secret things belong unto the LORD our God: but those things which are revealed belong unto us and to our children for ever, that we may do all the words of this law" (Deut. 29:29).

When two interpretations can be proposed for a given passage, the clearest should be accepted. The clear passage should interpret the obscure, not the obscure the clear.

Essential truth is not veiled by obscure and incidental passages. Essentials are not hidden mysteries. Everything necessary to salvation and Christian living is set forth clearly.

Application: How does the passage apply to me?

We may know what God says and how He says it. We may know what the Bible says and what it means, but it becomes of personal value only when we make a personal application. Application is the purpose of Bible study.

A Bible student may well ask the following questions to make his study relevant to life:

- What does the Bible say (*content*)?

- What does the Bible say to me (*personal application*)?

- What does the Bible say to me today (*relevant personal application*)?

103

- What am I going to do about it today (*immediate personal action on God's Word to me*)?

The will of the student is central to making Bible study relevant to life. J. H. Jowett wrote, "Get a will behind the eye, and the eye becomes a searchlight, and the familiar is made to disclose undreamed-of treasure." We must will to study, and as we study we must will to obey.

If we do not assimilate and appropriate Bible truth, spiritual atrophy will result. The immediate purpose of Bible study is to reproduce the experience that in the first place produced the Bible. A Chinese student, having caught this basic principle, wrote, "I am now reading the Bible *and behaving it.*" (See Mark 4:23–25.)

Example of Inductive Study

We are now ready to examine a portion of Scripture. Let us make a brief recap of some practical suggestions.

Approach the study hour with freshness of mind. Our best study is not done when we are weary mentally and physically.

Choose the passage. Read it over several times. Get a bird's-eye view of the whole; then explore the parts. Try to arrive at the intentions of the author. Find his purpose and note key words and expressions. What is each paragraph or unit of thought trying to say? Do paragraphs differ? How? What seems to be the thread of unity throughout? Search for this thread or chain. Connect the links of the chain.

Keep a record of all your observations, whether you

think they are significant or not. After you have noted the words or phrases that seem to reflect the author's purpose and have found the thread of thought, you are ready to search for outside help on problem passages, look at parallel passages, and compare geography, history, and the like.

Through the entire process it is of utmost importance to depend upon the Holy Spirit, without whom we cannot understand the Word of God.

Our sample inductive study passage will be Ephesians 1:3–14. This passage—a paragraph—is one long sentence of 268 words in the Revised Version and three sentences totaling 268 words in the King James. The passage contains a volume of truths and doctrines vital to Christian faith and practice.

These three sentences (King James Version)—one paragraph—bring a thread of truth regarding God's majestic plan of salvation. The thread can be noted in such phrases as "in Christ" (v. 3); "in him" (v. 4); "before him" (v. 4); "in whom" (v. 7).

A Study of Ephesians 1:3–14

Let's look at Ephesians 1:3–14 in a manner related to God's work on our behalf—past, present, and future. Words relating to our past are in *italic;* words relating to our present and future are in SMALL CAPS. The words used as threads of truth to connect are in regular type.

> *Blessed be the God and Father of our Lord Jesus Christ, who hath blessed us with all spiritual blessings in heavenly places* in Christ: *according as he hath chosen us* in him *before the foundation of the world,* THAT WE SHOULD BE HOLY AND

WITHOUT BLAME before him IN LOVE: *having predestinated us unto the adoption of children* by Jesus Christ TO HIMSELF, *according to the good pleasure of his will, to the praise of the glory of his grace, wherein he hath made us accepted* in the beloved.

In whom WE HAVE REDEMPTION through his blood, THE FORGIVENESS OF SINS, *according to the riches of his grace; wherein he hath abounded toward us in all wisdom and prudence; having made known unto us the mystery of his will, according to his good pleasure which he hath purposed* in himself: THAT IN THE DISPENSATION OF THE FULNESS OF TIMES HE MIGHT GATHER TOGETHER IN ONE ALL THINGS in Christ, BOTH WHICH ARE IN HEAVEN, AND WHICH ARE ON EARTH; EVEN in him: in whom *also we have obtained an inheritance, being predestinated according to the purpose of him who* WORKETH ALL THINGS AFTER THE COUNSEL OF HIS OWN WILL: THAT WE SHOULD BE TO THE PRAISE OF HIS GLORY, WHO FIRST TRUSTED in Christ.

In whom *ye also trusted, after that ye heard the word of truth, the gospel of your salvation:* in whom *also after that ye believed, ye were sealed with that holy Spirit of promise,* WHICH IS THE EARNEST OF OUR INHERITANCE UNTIL THE REDEMPTION OF THE PURCHASED POSSESSION, UNTO THE PRAISE OF HIS GLORY.

Paul launched into a subject—the song of salvation—so thrilling that he could scarcely pause for breath. The first sentence has eighty-nine words; the second, 125; and the last, fifty-four.

God the Father planned redemption for us. In

tribute to the Father (vv. 3–6), three of His acts on our behalf are mentioned: He chose us (v. 4); He adopted us (v. 5); He accepted us (v. 6). Acceptance is through the work and merit of the Beloved, His only begotten Son.

God the Son provided salvation for us. The second sentence of this passage pays tribute to the work of Christ (vv. 7–12): He redeemed us (v. 7); He has made known the mystery of His will (v. 9); He has granted us an inheritance (v. 11).

God the Holy Spirit has wrought salvation for us. He has given us a seal (v. 13), an earnest of our inheritance (v. 14), and a pledge of that perfect redemption that will be ours at Christ's coming (v. 14).

Each of these three tributes to the Trinity ends with the same expression—to the praise of His glory (vv. 6, 12, 14). All God's purposes center in Himself and are for His glory (Rom. 11:33).

Illustrative and Practical

Martin Luther said he studied the Bible in the way he gathered apples: He would first shake the whole tree so the ripest apples would fall. This he compared to study of the Bible as a whole. Next he would climb the tree and shake each limb, which is comparable to a survey of each book of the Bible. Then he would shake the branches, which is similar to chapter study. Next he would shake each twig—a picture of paragraph and sentence or verse study. Last, he would look under each leaf, comparing this to word study.

Research will supply us with meaningful information about the author, the scope, the occasion, the theme, the time, the place, and the form of writing.

With these helpful facts we can pick up the thread of truth and find God's purpose in a book.

There is a difference between interpretation and application. Some people arrive at far-fetched interpretations and applications because they fail to anchor to the proper meaning. Unwarranted thinking has led many to make applications without the foundation of proper interpretation.

The Bible is not a compendium of history. It contains history, but in only one place is there a display of historical technique (Luke 1:1–4). Biblical authority is not based on figures or dates. It is spiritual experience rather than historical record, reality in religion rather than statistical tables.

The Bible is not an outline of science. Religious life is as real as chemical reaction, but the Bible is recording it, not charting it.

The Bible is not merely literature. It is that, but it is more. The influence of the Bible as literature is great, but the content of the Bible is more to be considered than the excellence of the phrasing and the beauty of expression.

The Bible is not a code of ethics. It is "the only infallible rule of faith and conduct," but it is a spring of morality rather than a guide to morals.

The Bible shows us history that we may see God. It tells of nature that we may walk life's way with nature's God. It uses human words that we may hear the voice of God and see the Word made flesh.

108

Quick Quiz

• What is meant by inductive study? Compare it to synthetic study.

• What is meant by observation? Interpretation? Application?

• Why doesn't the Bible give a complete record of historical events?

• Name various ways of finding the meaning of a passage.

8

Study by Topics

It is important to understand the doctrines of the Bible.

Preliminary Consideration

Preview: Topical study is considered one of the most popular types of Bible study. By the use of a good concordance this type of study approach becomes one of the easier methods. An easy subject can be considered, or the scope of study may reach to the more difficult. Study by types and by biographies may be included under the general heading of topical study because of their similarities, but for purposes of this series they are separated.

A topical study of Christian doctrine is an important part of Bible study. Doctrinal truth is found in all the Bible. The more we study, the more we are amazed with the range of revealed truth. Doctrinal truth for the church is found for the most part in the New Testament but is foreshadowed in the Old.

Every Christian should study doctrine, for the entire structure of Christianity rests upon this foundation. The study of doctrine is not reserved for theologians. Paul states that the ministry gifts are given to perfect the church, "that we henceforth be no more children, tossed to and fro, and carried about with every wind of doctrine, by the sleight of men, and cunning craftiness, whereby they lie in wait to deceive" (Eph. 4:14).

Liberalism and neoorthodoxy have produced haziness of belief. Christians need clear-cut thinking regarding basic subjects on which God has dogmatically expressed Himself in His Word.

Objective: To set forth the values, procedures, and cautions of topical study of the Bible, with special emphasis on doctrine.

A Plan of Action

- Value
- Cautions
- Procedure
- Example

Value

Study by topics will do much to equip a person with a fundamental understanding of the great doctrines and principles of the Bible. There is error in teaching a doctrine with only a few selected texts, a practice followed by the false cults. When we gain proper emphasis and understanding of all that the Bible teaches on a given topic, we will be kept from error and grounded in the truth.

We feel it is important to know what great men

have to say on great subjects. Millions of Americans listen when the president outlines his program or makes an announcement affecting our welfare. If this is true, it is far more important to hear what God has to say on great subjects that have a bearing on us for all time and eternity. Too many people know only a part of what God has to say—usually only a small part—and so their knowledge is incomplete and their ideas are imperfect. We can know what God has to say on any topic only by going through the Bible and gathering information on what He has said.

Some people will accept only truth that a church recognizes. They accept the dogma of a church over the doctrines of the Bible. *Dogma* means "ecclesiastical recognition of a statement or tenet of belief embodied in a confession, creed, or statement of faith."

Others will accept no truth other than what natural human intellect can reason out. Still another group looks to visions, dreams, and operations of the gifts for spiritual direction.

There is, however, only one source for doctrine, "the all-sufficient rule for faith and practice." That is the Bible. Just as the Supreme Court of the United States is the final court of appeal, so too the Bible is the final authority for us. Dogmas, human reasonings, and supernatural manifestations are correct only as they agree with the Word of God.

Two words translated "doctrine" occur some fifty times in the New Testament. These two Greek words, *didache* and *didaskalia,* bear the meaning of "teaching, the work of a teacher, and the thing taught." *Doctrine* means "teaching or instruction," and it can be either good or bad. There are true doctrines and false doctrines.

We have a responsibility to understand the doctrines of the Bible (1 Tim. 4:6; Titus 2:7; Heb. 13:9). Paul emphasizes the need of "sound doctrine" (1 Tim. 1:10; 2 Tim. 4:3; Titus 1:9); "sound words" (2 Tim. 1:13); being "sound in the faith" (Titus 1:13); "wholesome words" (1 Tim. 6:3).

An important subject classified under topical study is Christian doctrine, thus the emphasis regarding this vital subject. We need not be greatly concerned about creeds and dogmas, but we must be concerned about doctrine, which is the foundation of Christ's church. Heresies would not gain such large followings if believers were rooted and grounded in Christian faith.

Myer Pearlman stated, "Strong beliefs make for strong character; clear-cut beliefs make for clear-cut character. Of course, a person's doctrinal belief is not his religion any more than the backbone is the man's personality. But as a good backbone is an essential part of a man's body, so a definite system of belief is an essential part of a man's religion."

Cautions

Topical study is not the only method of Bible study. If we follow this method exclusively, we will miss much that God has intended for us.

We must guard against studying only those topics that appeal to us. Jesus said, "Search the scriptures," and this is not done if we emphasize the study of certain portions only. Jesus meant *all the Bible*. There is a tendency with most of us to do those things that give us special delight. Many of us tend to overemphasize certain truths, or rather, fail to give proper emphasis to other areas of truth. To be physically healthy we must maintain a balanced diet. In like manner, we need a balanced spiritual diet by feeding on all the Word of God. To illustrate, some people are so taken up with the study of prophecy that they fail to have an interest in any other message of the Bible. This is true with other subjects as well.

Most of us can think of people who have made a nuisance of themselves because they are cranks on a few pet subjects. They are lopsided, for though they are well informed on their favorite topic, they are uninformed on many subjects equally as important.

To avoid a lack of balance, we should make topical study systematic. Let it be comprehensive and cover more than just a casual treatment of certain items.

Procedure

Topics of the Bible generally fall under the following classifications: 1) doctrines; 2) events; 3) places; 4) duties; 5) words; 6) biographies; 7) dispensations.

After choosing the topic to be studied, list all the passages that relate to the subject. Be thorough at this point. Find all that the Bible has to say on it. A good concordance, a topical textbook, and margin references will be very helpful. The followers of the cults err at this point. They are usually very free in quoting the Bible to prove their point, but they use isolated or selected texts without proper consideration of all the Bible has to say on the matter.

We must be exact as well as thorough. Determine the exact meaning of the passage with regard to the topic under study. Observe before you interpret. Study the meaning and usage of words.

The Bible dictionary and the margin translations are very helpful. Modern translations may also be used for the sake of comparison. Examine passages in the light of parallel passages and words in comparison to parallel words. A study of context, parallels, and word meanings will usually settle the meaning of a verse when it appears difficult. The meanings of many of the difficult passages in the Scriptures are made plain by other passages that throw light upon them.

After noting all that the Bible has to say on a subject and recording it on paper, the next task is to arrange the results. Usually we will have accumulated a large amount of material. Now we must get it into shape. The mere accumulation of many verses for the sake of being comprehensive is not enough. Verses should be chosen to make the subject clear and easily understood. The result should be an analysis, combining sufficiency of details with clarity of meaning.

Ever bear in mind the need for the help of the Holy Spirit. Those who have never known the touch of the Spirit are not certain that truth, real and complete, can be found. As the centuries have passed, one system of philosophy has followed another. Searchers after truth have found human systems to be incomplete and unsatisfying. But Jesus did not say truth would come by human searching and human intellect alone. Neither did He say that truth in its fullness would come in a moment. He did say, "If ye continue in my word, then are ye my disciples indeed; and ye shall know the truth..." (John 8:31–32). Jesus also said, "Thy word is truth" (John 17:17). The written Word reveals the Living Word. All who come face to face with Him in personal relationship realize He is pure truth. The Holy Spirit

116

comes to guide us into all truth (John 16:13).

Application must be made of what we have learned on the subject under study. The object of our study is not attained until the truth is applied in a manner to create a response. Bible truth must be translated into Christian living.

Example

The result of a study of the important subject of prayer is presented as an example of topical study.

The Doctrine of Prayer

Instances of mention

- The word *pray* occurs 292 times: Old Testament, 225 times; New Testament, sixty-seven times.

- The word *prayed* occurs sixty-five times: Old Testament, thirty-one times; New Testament, thirty-four times.

- The word *prayer* occurs 114 times: Old Testament, eighty-three times; New Testament, thirty-one times.

- The word *prayers* occurs twenty-four times: Old Testament, two times; New Testament, twenty-two times.

- The word *prayest* occurs two times in the New Testament.

- The word *prayeth* occurs seven times: Old Testament, four times; New Testament, three times.

- The word *praying* occurs twenty times: Old Testament, six times; New Testament, fourteen times.

Prayer is described as:

- Calling upon the name of the Lord (Gen. 12:8).
- Crying unto God (Ps. 27:7; 34:6).
- Drawing near to God (Ps. 73:28; Heb. 10:22).
- Looking up (Ps. 5:3).
- Lifting up the soul (Ps. 25:1).
- Lifting up the heart (Lam. 3:41).
- Pouring out the heart (Ps. 62:8).
- Pouring out the soul (1 Sam. 1:15).
- Crying to heaven (2 Chron. 32:20).
- Beseeching the Lord (Exod. 32:11).
- Seeking unto God (Job 8:5).
- Seeking the face of the Lord (Ps. 27:8).
- Making supplication (Job 8:5; Jer. 36:7).

Prayer is defined as:

- Communion (2 Cor. 3:18; 1 John 1:3).
- Supplication (Eph. 6:18; Phil. 4:6).
- Intercession (Rom. 8:26–27).
- Consisting of adoration, thanksgiving (Phil. 4:6), confession (James 5:16; 1 John 1:9), and petition (1 John 5:15).

Prayer is to be made:

- To God (Ps. 5:2).
- In the name of Jesus (John 14:13–14; 16:23–24).
- By the Holy Spirit (Rom. 8:26–27).
- At all times: night and day (1 Tim. 5:5); without ceasing (1 Thess. 5:17); always (2 Thess. 1:11); and continuing instant (Rom. 12:12).
- Everywhere (1 Tim. 2:8).
- Without hypocrisy and vain repetition (Matt. 6:5–7).
- Fervently (James 5:16; Col. 4:12).
- In faith (Matt. 21:22; Heb. 10:22; 11:1, 6; James 1:6; 1 John 5:14–15).
- With submission to God (Luke 22:42).

Posture in prayer:

- Standing (1 Kings 8:22; Mark 11:25)
- Bowing down (Ps. 95:6)
- Kneeling (2 Chron. 6:13; Ps. 95:6; Luke 22:41; Acts 20:36)
- Falling on the face (Num. 16:22; Josh. 5:14; 1 Chron. 21:16; Matt. 26:39)
- Spreading forth the hands (2 Chron. 6:13; Isa. 1:15)
- Lifting up the hands (Ps. 28:2; Lam. 2:19; 1 Tim. 2:8)

Answers to prayer are:

- Granted immediately at times (Isa. 65:24; Dan. 9:21–23).
- Delayed at times (Luke 18:7).

- Granted differently from our desires at times (2 Cor. 12:8–9).
- Granted beyond our expectation (Jer. 33:3; Eph. 3:20).

Answers are denied to those who:

- Regard iniquity in their heart (Ps. 66:18).
- Live in sin (Isa. 59:2; John 9:31).
- Ask amiss (James 4:3).
- Are wavering (James 1:6–7).
- Are self-righteous (Luke 18:10–14).

Summary and application

- Prayer, mentioned 524 times in the Bible, is very important.
- Prayer is made to the Father in the name of Jesus.
- We approach God with an attitude of worship, a sense of need, an assurance of faith, and submission to His will.
- We need to draw nigh to God in prayer, placing ourselves at His disposal, so He might channel His creative faith through us.

Prayer implies the existence of God and the responsibility of man; it has no meaning for those who deny either. It is more natural that God in His great mercy should answer the prayers of His children than that earthly parents should grant the requests of their children (Matt. 7:11).

Illustrative and Practical

Topical study was D. L. Moody's favorite method of Bible study. He once gave several days to the study of "grace." When he had finished he was so full of the subject that he rushed out on the street and said to the first man he met, "Do you know anything about grace?"

"Grace who?" asked the man.

"The grace of God that bringeth salvation," replied Moody, and he began to pour out to that man the rich treasures he had dug out of the Bible.

Some don'ts: Don't convince yourself as to what the Bible says before you study it. Let the Bible reveal itself. Don't decide your doctrine first and then turn to the Bible to ratify it. Let the Bible teach you.

A French Unitarian minister said, "Purity of heart and life is more important than correctness of opinion." Another French preacher answered him thus, "Healing is more important than the remedy, but without the remedy there would be no healing." There is more to living the Christian life than merely knowing Christian doctrine, but there would be no Christian life and experience if there were no Christian doctrine.

What one gets from art or music or the Bible depends very largely upon what one brings to them. To come to these with a tired body, an ignorant mind, and an unsympathetic spirit is to rob them of much of their power and meaning. And in the case of the Bible, the crux of all true study is the purpose and practice of applying any truths, any suggestions for good that we may gain from it, immediately and

121

persistently to life. We need not only to read the Book, but in the words of Ezekiel, to "eat it." (See Ezekiel 3:1–3.) Let the Word enter the bloodstream of our personalities until it becomes bone of our bone and flesh of our flesh.

Not long before he died, Sir Walter Scott called out, "Bring me the Book."

"What book, sir?" asked John Garlock.

"There is but one Book," replied the great Scotsman, "the Bible."

It is *the* Book; no other is like it in its appeal, its satisfying message, and its gripping power. No other will stand such rereading and study; it is different.

Quick Quiz

• What are the advantages of topical study?

• List errors to avoid in topical study.

• What is meant by doctrine? Why is its study important?

* What tools aid in topical study?

• Define prayer.

Now all these things happened unto them for ensamples.

—1 CORINTHIANS 10:11

Matthew 12:39
John 20:25
Romans 4:11
2 Corinthians 3:6
Galatians 4:24
Colossians 2:16–17
Titus 2:7
Hebrews 8:4–5; 9:23–24; 10:1;
   11:19
1 Peter 3:21
Revelation 11:8

9

Study by Types

Study of the New Testament is enriched by the Old Testament persons, objects, and events that, by God's providence, were planned to foreshadow something higher in the Christian era.

Preliminary Consideration

Preview: The Bible abounds with figures of speech such as metaphors, similes, parables, allegories, symbols, and types. These forms of speech were not used in Holy Writ as a result of the fancies of men; they were recorded as the authors were moved by the Holy Spirit.

God has chosen to represent spiritual things by means of natural things. The study of types becomes a blessing that greatly enriches us in our understanding of spiritual truths. Large portions of the Old Testament become meaningful as we understand their typical meaning. Exodus and Leviticus open to those who see their intent and purpose as revealed in the antitypes of the New Testament. The writers of the New Testament interpret the Old Testament by explaining its types.

God the Father has seemingly taken great delight in setting forth truth, particularly the marvels of the person and work of His Son, by many illustrations and word pictures. The search for those that are in type form is a very interesting form of Bible study.

Modernists may object to the study of types in the light of their rejection of the Old Testament as anything but an old story book of the Jews, but type study opens new vistas of Bible truth to earnest students.

Objective: To create an interest in the study of typology and find scriptural rules governing this fascinating form of Bible study.

A Plan of Action

- What is a type?
- Why study types?
- Cautions and rules
- Kinds of types

What Is a Type?

The word *type* does not appear in the English Bible with the exception of a margin reference on 1 Corinthians 10:11, where the word translated "ensamples" is shown to mean types. On the other hand, the word *tupos,* from which we get our word *type,* occurs sixteen times in the New Testament. For example, it is rendered "print" (John 20:25); "figures" (Acts 7:43); "fashion" (Acts 7:44); "manner" (Acts 23:25); "figure" (Rom. 5:14); "form" (Rom. 6:17); "examples" (1 Cor. 10:6); "ensamples" (1 Cor. 10:11;

1 Thess. 1:7; 1 Pet. 5:3); "ensample" (Phil. 3:17; 2 Thess. 3:9); "example" (1 Tim. 4:12); and "pattern" (Titus 2:7; Heb. 8:5). Literally it means "stamp" or "impress."

Eight words are used to set forth the antitype or reality to which the type corresponds. They are "figure" (1 Pet. 3:21); "body" (Col. 2:17); "very image" (Heb. 10:1); "good things to come" (Heb. 10:1); "things in the heavens" (Heb. 9:23); "the true" (Heb. 9:24); "the spirit" (2 Cor. 3:6); and "spiritually" (Rev. 11:8).

Possibly the best definition of the word *type* is given by Paul in his letter to the Colossians, "a shadow of things to come" (Col. 2:17; cf. Heb. 10:1). A *type* is a "God-ordained means of communicating truth in illustrative form." In other words, behind the historical interpretation of the Scriptures where the word or series of words is used, there lies the spiritual. The brazen serpent on the pole is a part of the historical record during Israel's wanderings, but it presents, in type, the death of Jesus (Num. 21:9).

To say that one thing is a type of another requires more than mere resemblance. Not only must the former resemble the latter, but it must be *designed* to resemble it. This then becomes the relationship of the type and the antitype. *Antitype* literally means "answering the type."

A type involves three things: 1) an outward object or thing that represents a higher thing; 2) the higher thing, which is called the antitype or the reality; 3) the work of the type, which the Bible calls "a shadow." A type is a sign, an example, a pattern, a figure. A parable is an earthly story with a heavenly meaning; a type is a visible, earthly thing that the Lord has designed to teach us an invisible, heavenly, or spiritual thing. The type is the shadow; the antitype is the substance.

An *allegory* is a double representation in words; a *type* is a double representation in action. In a type the literal is intended and is planned to represent the spiritual. Another outward representation of spiritual truth is the *symbol.* As a rule, the symbol illustrates that which already exists, whereas the type prefigures that which is to come. In popular usage the words *type, symbol,* and *illustration* are interchangeable terms. But in the Old Testament a type is more restricted in usage than either a symbol or an illustration.

The study of typology is closely associated with the study of prophecy. Almost every type has something of a prophetic nature. A type prefigures a coming reality, while prophecy foretells it. Typology and prophecy, while holding marked similarities, are separate methods of setting forth truth. Typology uses representative persons, places, institutions, and symbols, whereas prophecy uses figurative language.

Types, for the most part, relate to redemption, either as to the person and work of Christ or to the believer. Some relate to the Holy Spirit and the church.

The Pentateuch contains most of the types. Some are in the historical books; few, if any, are to be found in the poetical and prophetical books. This is to be expected. The great truths of redemption must be set forth in the early books, but as the revelation of redemption proceeds, types give way to the spoken word of the prophets. The great typological teachings become the basis for the flaming ministry of the prophets, for they spoke of a redemption acted upon but yet to come.

Why Study Types?

First Corinthians 10:11 tells us concerning the wilderness experiences of the Israelites, that "all these things happened unto them for ensamples [types]." Paul explains that the record of these events is given to us for the purpose of teaching us lessons. This would include the events from the deliverance out of Egyptian bondage to the time of coming into the land of promise. These were actual events, but they had deep spiritual meaning for New Testament saints.

Sir Robert Anderson declared, "The typology of the Old Testament is the very alphabet of the language in which the doctrine of the New Testament is written, and as many of our great theologians are admittedly ignorant of the typology, we need not feel surprised if they are not always the safest exponents of the doctrines."

The early books of the Bible present a series of pictures to which reference and explanation is made in the New Testament. It is to be regretted that many people read the New Testament without any reference to or understanding of the types of the Old Testament. St. Augustine said:

> The New is in the Old contained;
> The Old is in the New explained.

Typology must be studied within the boundaries of certain principles. It is scriptural to study this subject, for the writers of Scripture and the Lord Himself made so many references that used types for teaching great lessons. As the surgeon's knife is of greatest value in the hands of the surgeon, so the Bible is most effectively used by those who are skilled in its interpretation. Those who wish to explore the great spiritual applications of the Pentateuch and other portions of the Old Testament will find a study of types to be almost a must to accomplish such an end. The Holy Spirit uses the things that are seen to illumine and teach us the things that are unseen.

The Old Testament types were for the purpose of illustrating or throwing light on the great precepts and doctrines revealed in the New Testament. The type is insufficient in itself, but it throws light on the gem of New Testament truth, causing the light to shine into our minds as the Holy Spirit makes application to our spiritual intelligence.

Types were given for the purpose of manifesting that which pertained to the Law of Moses, preparing the way for the fuller and better things in the antitype. All that pertained to the Old Covenant was but temporary as a forerunner or preparation for the better things in the New Covenant. Every type is but the shadow of which the antitype is the substance.

The study of types is important for several reasons:

- The Holy Spirit placed types in Scripture (Exod. 26:33; Mark 15:38; Heb. 9:6–9; 10:19–22).

- Jesus Himself constantly referred to types. Take note of types in the Gospel of John alone: John 1:14, the antitype of the tabernacle; 1:29, the fulfillment of the Old Testament sacrifices. Christ compares Himself to the temple (2:19); to the brazen serpent (3:14); to the manna (6:31–35); as the antitype of the Old Testament shepherds (10:11); as the corn of wheat that brought forth the sheaf of the firstfruits (12:24); as the laver (13:10); as the true Vine (15:1); as the Great High Priest (chapter 17).

- Paul declares that Israel's experiences in the wilderness—covering a lengthy portion of Scripture—"happened unto them for ensamples [types]" (1 Cor. 10:11).

- Typology is another evidence of the essential unity of the Bible. The two Testaments are united in relating the great plan of redemption. Both must be the product of the same mind, for they are intertwined in one great plan to present the eternal purpose of God.

Cautions and Rules

Some have taken the study of types far beyond the realm of sensible interpretation. This area of study can be very helpful, but it demands mental restraint and controlled imagination. To allow the mind to be undisciplined at this point is to become open to fanaticism.

There are rules that govern the study of types. The writers of Holy Writ never destroyed the historical sense of Scripture to establish the spiritual. Bear in mind that doctrines are not built on types. Our doctrinal beliefs are founded on the statements of God's Word and are illustrated by types. We cannot arbitrarily set something forth as a type merely because of resemblance.

131

The Bible clearly defines many types. For example, the "law having a shadow of good things to come" (Heb. 10:1); "Adam...who is the figure of him that was to come" (Rom. 5:14). Canaan is pictured as a figure of "a better country, that is, an heavenly" (Heb. 11:16). The tabernacle of Moses, with its priesthood, offerings, and furnishings, is set forth as a figure of great typological teaching (Heb. 9:8–11).

The Bible indicates other types by an interchange of names between the type and the antitype. As illustrations, note that Christ is called "the last Adam" (1 Cor. 15:45), "the Lamb of God" (John 1:29), or "our passover" (1 Cor. 5:7).

Another warrant for a type is found where an evident analogy exists between some Old Testament event, person, or object and the spiritual truth to which it points in the New Testament. Examples include Joseph as a type of Christ; Jonah and the whale illustrating the death, burial, and resurrection of Christ; and Israel's experiences from Egypt to Canaan as a type of the Christian life.

The Passover is a type of the Lord's supper. Circumcision is a type of baptism. Leprosy is a type of sin and its pollution. Hagar and Ishmael are types of the covenant of works.

A last and very important rule for types is to recognize that as there is similitude between the type and the antitype, there is also dissimilitude. We fall into error when we try to make details typological. Adam was a type of Christ, but the last Adam infinitely surpassed the first Adam. Jonah was a type of Christ in the one experience of being in the fish for three days. No type is total.

Kinds of Types

There are several helpful ways of grouping types. Someone has said that Genesis has the dispensational types; Exodus, the redemption types; Leviticus, the sacrificial types; Numbers, the wilderness types; Joshua, the Canaan types; the historical books, the kingdom types; and the prophets, the prophetic types. All types fall into three general groups: 1) persons; 2) ceremonies; 3) historical events.

Persons

1. Adam—a type of Christ (Rom. 5:14): As head of creation (Gen. 1:26; 2:19–20; Ps. 8:3–6; Heb. 2:5–9); as head of the race—the first Adam of the fallen race, the last Adam of the redeemed (Rom. 5:12, 17); as head over Eve (Gen. 2:21–24; Eph. 5:25–32)—the first Adam and his bride were one flesh (Gen. 2:24); the last Adam and His bride are one spirit (1 Cor. 6:17).

2. Abel—his blood cried for vengeance (Gen. 4:10); Christ's blood speaks for pardon (Heb. 12:24).

3. Enoch—a type of the saints who are to be translated (Gen. 5:24; Heb. 11:5; 1 Thess. 4:14–17).

4. Noah—a type of the Jewish people, left on the earth but preserved through the

Great Tribulation (Gen. 6:9; Jer. 30:5–9; Rev. 12:13–16).

5. Melchizedek—a type of Christ the King-priest (Gen. 14:18; Heb. 6:20; 7:1–4, 23–24).

6. Isaac—a type of Christ "obedient unto death" (Gen. 22:1–10; Phil. 2:5–8) and of Christ as the Bridegroom of a called-out bride (Gen. 24).

7. Moses—a type of Christ as Prophet (Deut. 18:15–19; Acts 3:19–23).

8. Aaron—a type of Christ as Priest (Exod. 28:1; Heb. 2:17; 5:1–5).

9. David—a type of Christ as King (Isa. 55:3; Acts 13:26–37).

10. Jonah—a type of Christ's death, burial, and resurrection (Jon. 1:17; Matt. 12:39–41).

Abraham typifies many characteristics of the father-hood of God. Jacob illustrates the special leading of God, and Joseph presents a full picture of Christ as the Beloved of the Father. Elijah is a type of John the Baptist. In many points, Joshua, Samson, Solomon, Elisha, Zerubbabel, and Joshua the high priest are types of Christ.

Numerous groups or orders of persons are types. Among these are the Nazarites, the Jewish nation, the "firstborn," the prophets, the priests, and the kings.

Ceremonies

1. The Passover (Exod. 12; John 19:32–36; 1 Cor. 5:7; 1 Pet. 1:18–19)

2. The tabernacle (Heb. 9:1–28). Exodus and Leviticus abound with types found in the tabernacle and offerings. Great doctrines are typified in the furnishings of the tabernacle (Exod. 25–40). Incarnation is illustrated in the veil, justification at the altar, sanctification at the laver, intercession at the golden altar, worship in the holy of holies, communion at the table, and reconciliation at the mercy seat. The table of shewbread, the ark of the covenant, and the golden candlesticks are types. Among the many other ceremonial types are the offerings—the burnt offering, the sweet savour offering, the meal offering, the peace offering, the sin offering, and the trespass offering. These are rich with spiritual truth as they portray the atoning work of the Lord Jesus Christ (Lev. 1–7).

3. Other significant types are portrayed by the consecration of the priests (Exod. 28–29; Lev. 8–9) and the cleansing of the leper (Lev. 13–14). Ceremonial acts such as circumcision and the laws of purification are typological. Then there are the festivals (Lev. 23): the feast of the Passover, showing forth redemption; the feast of unleavened bread, a holy walk; the feast

135

of firstfruits, resurrection; the feast of Pentecost, the outpouring of the Holy Spirit; the feast of trumpets, symbols of testimony; the day of atonement and the feast of tabernacles, both a memorial and prophetic feast like the Lord's supper. Other ceremonial types include the sabbaths (seventh day and seventh year) and the year of Jubilee (Lev. 25).

Historical Events

The miraculous experiences of the children of Israel in their journey from Egypt to Canaan are specifically declared to be types of the believer from the time he comes under the protection of the sprinkled blood until he enters into the promised rest (1 Cor. 10:11; Heb. 3:7–4:11). The most prominent types during this journey are:

1. The Passover—redemption by blood (Exod. 12; Eph. 1:7).

2. The Red Sea—leaving the world behind (Exod. 14; Gal. 1:4; 6:14).

3. The tabernacle—access to God (Exod. 25; Heb. 10).

4. Manna and water—provision (Exod. 16–17; John 6–7).

5. Perils—a grumbling and critical spirit (Num. 20:3); unbelief (Exod. 13–14); backsliding (Num. 14:4); compromise (Josh. 9).

6. Victory through faith in God and obedience to His Word (Josh. 1).

Other historical places and incidents, rich in typological meaning, include the burning bush (Exod. 3; Acts 7:30); Mount Sinai; and the cities of refuge (Josh. 20). This is but a partial list.

Illustrative and Practical

The Bible is:

B–eautiful when we	**B**–ehold it
I–nteresting when we	**I**–nvestigate it
B–lessed	**B**–elieve it
L–ife-giving and we should	**L**–ive by it
E–ternal and we should	**E**–xtol it

The typological portions of the Bible are very important. Jehovah God designed to express His great thought of redemption to His chosen people Israel in a symbolic manner. By laws, ceremonies, institutions, events, and persons He tried to keep before them the hope of a coming Redeemer. The Lord Jesus Christ is the key to Moses. As we compare type and antitype we learn the glories of salvation provided through the Redeemer to whom and around whom all Scripture centers.

Vast numbers of people go to great effort and expense to travel to far corners of the world to visit shrines, temples, mausoleums, and pyramids. They feel well repaid as they behold the grandeur and greatness of a past civilization. In the Bible we have pictured for us a building not made with human hands. It is the church, whose Founder and Head is on the right hand of the Father in heaven. This great building and its design is set forth in shadow and type in glorious beauty in the Old Testament. The God who indwells the church today dwelt among His people in the tabernacle of Moses. It is fascinating to study that tabernacle wherein dwelt the *shekinah*, the manifested glory of the living God. The tabernacle with its appointments, persons, and ceremonies fully disclosed the plan of redemption.

A type is called a *shadow*. We cannot have a shadow unless there is an object to cast a shadow. The shadow is visible because of light. We need the enlightenment of the Holy Spirit to see Christ as the body that casts the shadows we see in the Old Testament Scriptures. The Passover lamb is simply a shadow cast by the Lamb of God who takes away the sin of the world. The brazen serpent on a pole is only a shadow cast by the cross on Golgotha's hill.

Quick Quiz

- What is a type?

- Where do types appear?

- State some cautions and rules regarding types.

- What persons and objects of the New Testament are generally foreshadowed?

- Name some of the more prominent types in the three general groups of persons, ceremonies, and historical events.

Elias was a man subject to like passions as we are.

—JAMES 5:17

Genesis 32:9–32
1 Corinthians 10:11

10

Study by Biographies

Bible biographies are intensely human. They give us courage, instruction, example, and warning as followers of God.

Preliminary Consideration

Preview: Human life is a most interesting fact in the world. The study of people is one of the most fascinating studies we can undertake. It is the human element that has appeal in every work of art, in every news story, in every event of daily life. Thought life centers around people.

Abstract principles take on meaning as they relate to life and find expression in the thoughts and actions of persons. Ideals must come down to earth and walk in the guise of men to become useful and reasonable.

The study of the lives of great men and women has always been a source of inspiration and help to succeeding generations. Longfellow wrote in "A Psalm of Life":

Lives of great men all remind us
We can make our lives sublime,
And, departing, leave behind us
Footprints on the sands of time;
Footprints, that perhaps another,
Sailing o'er life's solemn main,
A forlorn and shipwrecked brother,
Seeing, shall take heart again.

The Bible is a book of fascinating biographies. God has chosen to give much of His Word in biographical form with divine purpose. When we live with Bible characters in their environments, their lives become meaningful to us. The narratives are rich in devotional lessons, applicable in everyday life. Basic principles are clearly set forth in a divine-human relationship.

Objective: This lesson will show the blessing and value of study by biography and will lay down principles to follow in this method of Bible study.

A Plan of Action

- Value
- Principles
- Example

Value

Mary Petrie says in her book, *Clues to Holy Writ,* that the Bible is literature in its four most interesting forms. They are biographies, the word pictures of outstanding men; letters, the utterances of the heart; poetry, the loftiest thinking of men; and history, philosophy exemplified.

In proportion to its size, no book offers so large a collection of literature in which so many different persons appear as does the Bible. There are 2,930 separate persons mentioned in the Bible. Many of these are mentioned only by name, but hundreds of them furnish material for biographical study.

Biographical study is the most common method used in teaching children. Where is the person who did not thrill to the stories of Bible characters in his childhood? Children have vivid pictures of baby Moses in the ark, of David with his slingshot, and of Daniel in the lions' den. Little girls love the stories of Mary, Ruth, Esther, and the baby Jesus. Adults also profit from biographical study.

Since God chose to use biography so extensively, and since all that He does has purpose, these biographies have meaning for us. They are recorded "for our admonition" (1 Cor. 10:11). Knowledge of the persons of the Bible is necessary if we are to understand the Bible. It is both a privilege and a duty for us to make a study of Bible biographies.

The characters pictured in the Bible graphically portray the story of the heart of man. All types are represented. They are not so idealized that they become irrelevant to life in their times or the problems of life situations in our day. These persons were real men and women, "of like passions as we are" (James 5:17). The Bible sets forth men of like human clay. They are not flawless saints.

God does not hide the fact that many of the greatest men of the Bible were guilty of folly and sin. The story is often delineated very frankly. Some of these men ascended to great heights of devotion and service, but at other times they fell into the depths of sin. God does not cover up for His people. He presents men who knew human struggle and failure.

David is a representative illustration. It is said of him that he was a man after God's own heart. Yet on occasion David was a liar, an adulterer, and a murderer. This does not mean that God condones sin. David was a man after God's own heart in that he repented of his sin and found God's pardon. The frailty of Bible men does not give us license to sin. These men were for types and examples, and their story is "written for our admonition, upon whom the ends of the world are come" (1 Cor. 10:11).

There is no glossing over the weaknesses or sins of the great and the good. The Bible records the duplicity of Abraham the upright man, the anger of Moses the meek man, the weakness of Samson the powerful man, the fear of Elijah the bold man, the carnality of David the devoted man, the folly of Solomon the wise man, and the failure of Peter the rocklike man.

The records of men are helpful because they are complete transparencies. Every portrait is faithfully realistic and instructive. Most paintings are of good men; some are of evil persons such as Absalom, Jezebel, Ahab, and Judas. Good or bad, all are pictured objectively as warnings to us.

Bible biographies help to clear up moral and religious problems. Abstract discussions are of little help to men. But relate the matter to an expression of personal struggle and the picture changes. Take Peter, for example. Separate the moral and spiritual aspects of his character from his personal struggle, and men think of it as so much theory. Relate these, and his life is relevant to ours.

We must take into account God's true estimate of

the men of the Bible. This will not lower these men in our thinking; rather, it will magnify the grace of God and encourage us. The biographies of the Bible have a spiritual value above all other biographies, for they relate to us the reactions of the human nature to divine matters. From these lessons we learn how to avoid similar pitfalls and to better adjust our lives to the will of God and harvest the great blessings of obedience to His will.

The study of Bible biographies has yet another value. God has chosen to reveal His plan and purpose through representative men. A knowledge of the persons of the Bible is necessary if we are to understand the Bible. If we are to understand Genesis, the foundation book of the Bible, we must know and understand God's dealings with ten representative men—Adam, Cain, Abel, Seth, Enoch, Noah, Abraham, Isaac, Jacob, and Joseph.

Principles

There are several principles, or guidelines, to follow when engaging in Bible study by biography. The following list may prove too all-inclusive for some cases, but it will be a guide suggesting certain factors for which to watch.

- As a first step, assemble all the references on the character to be studied. These references are often found scattered throughout the Bible. The bulk of the information may be found in one chapter or in a consecutive series of chapters. An isolated mention elsewhere in the Bible may contribute a great deal to our insight of the person's character. The New Testament has many enlightening statements that are clues to the importance of Old Testament persons.

- Guard against confusing references relating to two or more persons having the same name. All persons must be accurately identified. To illustrate, there are six Marys mentioned in the New Testament—the virgin Mary (Matt. 1:18); Mary Magdalene (Matt. 27:56); Mary of Bethany (John 11:1); Mary, the wife of Cleophas (John 19:25); Mary, mother of John Mark (Acts 12:12); and Mary of Rome (Rom. 16:6). There are four or five men named John, at least three named James, and eight who bear the name Judas. In the Old Testament there are thirty men by the name of Zechariah, twenty named Nathan, and fifteen called Jonathan. The Bible lists only one Isaac, one Moses, one David, one Solomon, and one Isaiah. There is one Abraham and one Jacob, but the former was called Abram and the latter was renamed Israel. On the other hand, Peter had more than one name, being also called Simon, Cephas, and by his surname Bar-jona.

- Determine the meaning of the person's name. Bible names are meaningful; they often express some significant characteristic. Jacob's name, meaning "supplanter," was changed to Israel, meaning "a prince with God." God did this with purpose; it was not coincidence.

- Much can be learned by noting the background of the character under study. Trace his ancestry if possible. Did he have an education, such as Moses or Paul, or did he come from a background such as Peter possessed? Where did he spend his early years? What influences were brought to bear upon him in his youth? Timothy, for instance, possessed a godly heritage, which he received from his grandmother, Lois, and his mother, Eunice.

- A study of the friends and associates of the character will prove helpful. Take David and Jonathan as an illustration.

- Take note of the places where the life story of the man unfolds. Moses' life is in three divisions of forty years each—forty years among royalty in Egypt, forty years in Midian, and finally forty years of leading the Israelites in the wilderness. Several of Paul's epistles become all the more meaningful when we realize they were written from a Roman prison. His declaration in Philippians 4:11 "that I have learned, in whatsoever state I am, therewith to be content" is a triumphant testimonial coming from a vibrant missionary traveler confined in a prison. Oftentimes outstanding events in the lives of Bible men center around places of crises.

- Observe particular traits of character displayed in the varying situations of life. Paul,

147

Peter, and John were strong leaders in the church. It is interesting to note how God used their particular traits to present His truths. Each sets forth one of the three cardinal graces of faith, hope, and love. Paul can be called the apostle of faith; his epistles are epistles of faith. In like manner, Peter is the apostle of hope, as revealed in his letters. John, the beloved disciple, writes of love in his letters as the apostle of love. Jacob is another whose particular character traits shine through in the events of his life. And what of Peter, with his impetuous spirit?

- List his failures, faults, and shortcomings. What were the steps leading to failure? How did his failures affect his future?

- Attempt to determine the great crisis in the life of the character. How did he react?

- Find the contributions made by the individual, contributions to his day and to ours.

- What is the main lesson of his life, and what is its particular value to us?

Example

A biographical study is made of Jacob according to the guidelines listed above. Jacob's life is particularly helpful as a character study. Many other Bible characters seem almost faultless. Men like Abraham, Joseph, Moses, Elijah, Elisha, Stephen, Paul, and

John almost reach perfection. But Jacob was a man with faults. We are so much like him. The study of his life helps us to know that if God's grace and power can transform a deceiver such as Jacob into a prince having power with men and God, surely there is hope for us!

References
Space does not permit a listing of all Bible references to Jacob. Mention is made of him 390 times—366 times in the Old Testament, twenty-four in the New.

Name
Jacob means "supplanter" (Gen. 25:26). His name was changed to *Israel,* which means "a prince with God" (Gen. 32:28).

Ancestry
Jacob was the son of Isaac and grandson of Abraham, who was the father of God's chosen people. Abraham, in turn, was a direct descendant of Noah through the line of Shem. Jacob and Esau were twin sons of Isaac and Rebekah. Jacob, the younger, superseded Esau, an arrangement contrary to natural tribal law. Jacob wronged Esau by gaining his birthright and blessing. Spurgeon's analysis of the deception was that here were three good people— Isaac, Rebekah, and Jacob—who fell into sin simply because as a family they lacked mutual respect and confidence. Isaac craftily arranged for Esau to prepare a banquet (Gen. 27:1–4); Rebekah plotted to foil Isaac (Gen. 27:5–10); and Jacob's lack of faith in God to fulfill His word caused him to be a deceiver (Gen. 25:23; 27:11–24).

Friends and associates

Because of his deceit and treachery, Jacob had to flee from home and friends. He found refuge with his uncle Laban. Here he served fourteen years for the hand of Rachel. His wages were changed ten times in twenty years.

Places

Jacob's life unfolds in four places. He was a deceiver and supplanter in Beersheba; a servant in Haran, still deceiving and being deceived; a saint in Hebron after his meeting with God at Peniel; and a seer in Egypt.

Traits of character

By nature Jacob was a supplanter. While he did wrong, at the same time he had set his heart on that which God had promised. He believed in the value of both the birthright and the blessing. He had an appreciation for spiritual values. While Jacob was shrewd, he was not bold. His approach to things was more that of a fox than of a lion. He slyly deceived; he fled from home rather than face Esau; and he "stole away unawares to Laban" when he fled from him (Gen. 31:20). But he was changed, as we shall see.

Failures

Jacob tricked Esau out of his birthright (Gen. 25:29–34). He stole the blessing by deceiving Isaac (Gen. 27:1–33). He outwitted Laban with the cattle (Gen. 30:25–43). Jacob continued to deceive until he was transformed at Peniel. But he continued to reap for his wrongdoing. He lived as an exile and had a sad harvest of his evil years. There was the dishonor of his daughter Dinah (Gen. 34), the death of his beloved Rachel (Gen. 35:16–20), the supposed death of the favored Joseph (Gen. 37), and the shame of Judah (Gen. 38).

Great crisis of life

Jacob's great crisis was at Peniel. Twenty years passed between Jacob's experience with God at Bethel and his experience at Peniel where he wrestled with God. When Jacob submitted, his name was changed to *Israel,* a prince with God.

Contributions

Jacob contributed much to Israel and to us. His experiences vividly bear out Paul's statement to the Galatians: "Be not deceived; God is not mocked: for whatsoever a man soweth, that shall he also reap" (Gal. 6:7).

Lesson for us

God's blessings and prosperity do not always prove that all is right with a child of God. Jacob prospered when with Laban. God was gracious to him despite his machinations. God commanded Jacob to return to the land of promise. There he would face Esau, who had murder in his heart. It is an evidence of the faith of Jacob that he recognized God's voice and was willing to obey, even though he knew to submit to God's will was to risk his life and all that he possessed. Jacob had endured a long period of discipline in Haran, but the old nature still needed more change. At Peniel, God brought him to a conflict and crisis that became the great and final turning point of his life. Only after that was he able to face Esau and

151

enter Canaan in the manner God wanted.

W. G. Scroggie summarizes the biography of Jacob in the Book of Genesis as follows:

I. The supplanter at Beersheba—well of the oath (25:19–28:22)
A. The birthright (25:19–34)
B. The blessing (27–28)
  1. The deceit of Rebekah and Jacob (27:1–29)
  2. The determination of Esau (27:50–45)
  3. The departure for Haran (27:46–28:22)

II. The servant at Haran—very dry, or parched (29:1–31:55)
A. Jacob deceived (29:1–30:24)
  1. Jacob's contract (29:1–19)
  2. Jacob cheated (29:20–30)
  3. Jacob's children (29:31–30:24)
B. Jacob deceiving (30:25–31:55)
  1. Laban's cattle (30:25–43)
  2. Laban's charge (31:1–42)
  3. Laban's covenant (31:43–55)

III. The saint at Hebron—fellowship (32:1–45:28)
A. Discipleship (32:1–33:20)
  1. The consternation of Jacob (32:1–21)
  2. The conflict at Peniel (32:22–32)
  3. The conciliation of Esau (33)
B. Discipline (34:1–45:28)
  1. In the dishonor done to Dinah (34)
  2. In the deaths of Rachel and Isaac (35)
  3. In the destruction (supposed) of Joseph (37)

4. In the disgrace of Judah (38)
5. In the departure of Benjamin (43)

IV. The seer in Egypt—land of depression
(46:1–49:33)
A. Prophetic blessing on the two sons (48)
B. Prophetic blessing of the twelve sons (49)

Illustrative and Practical

The influence of a great life

An old man stood before the tablet commemorating General Booth in the humble room where he met the poor and prayed them into the kingdom of God. "Can a man say his prayers here?" the old man asked. He was told that he could, and he knelt and said, "O God, do it again; do it again!"

The Christian is a reflector

There is a wonderful difference in men, even good men. If a ball of glowing hot iron be placed before a metallic reflector, it will throw back the heat with great power; but if placed before a glass mirror, light will be reflected, but no heat. Christians are reflectors, but they differ greatly in their reflecting power. All virtuous traits of character are but reflections caught from Christ. Yet some of these traits are developed more powerfully in some Christians than in others. John prominently reflected love; Paul, zeal; reconverted Peter, courage; Cornelius, devotion; and Dorcas, benevolence. The power of reflection depends upon the nearness of the object to the mirror. If, then, we desire to show forth much of Christ, we must walk close to Him.

Life portraits in the Bible

The saga of human friendship is sung in the story of David and Jonathan.

The love of a husband and wife is beautifully portrayed in Jacob and Rachel. Fourteen years of servitude were as a few days for the love he bore her. Dying lonely and sorrowful, long years afterward, his thoughts were of her.

Note the many pictures of home life—the hospitable home of Mary, Martha, and Lazarus in Bethany; the widow of Nain and her son.

The frailties of man are portrayed—Judas the traitor, Peter who lost his head in a crisis, Balaam the prophet who was false for greed or gain.

Study the leaders of men. There is Abraham, who founded a race and pioneered a religion, and Moses, who built a nation out of slaves. Thrill to the story of Paul, the great missionary and theologian.

The Bible contains the biographies of many people—Cain, Methuselah, Isaac, Ishmael, Joseph, Samson, Samuel, Jezebel, Elijah, Abigail, Gamaliel, Dorcas, Demas, Barnabas, Peter, John. Choose one and begin an exciting study.

Quick Quiz

• What are the values of biographical study?

• Why does the Bible not gloss over the failures of great men?

• Name several principles to follow in biographical study.

• Why are names and places important in Bible study?

• What lessons are to be learned from Jacob?

O how I love thy law! it is my meditation all the day.

—Psalm 119:97

Psalm 119

11

Chapters...Verses...Words

God reveals Himself through the words of His Word.

Preliminary Consideration

Preview: The original text of the Bible had no chapter and verse divisions. The division into chapters was introduced by Stephen Langton, who later became archbishop of Canterbury. These divisions were made about A.D. 1250 in the Latin text. Verse divisions were made many years later. These are very helpful to us in locating and identifying Scripture passages. The chapter divisions are not quite perfect as to units of thought, but they are fairly satisfactory. For example, the theme of the well-known fifty-third chapter of Isaiah really begins with the last three verses of the preceding chapter. Most of the 1,189 chapters in the Bible are just long enough to read for morning devotions.

There is a vast difference between merely reading a chapter and reading it with understanding. To get the most benefit from chapter study, we should find an outline. When we have established this, we can then begin to think our way through a book, chapter by chapter.

The study of the Bible by verses also brings us to an area of rich possibilities. Some verses are historical in nature; others are doctrinal, expository, narrative, or descriptive.

The study of words is another enriching experience. We believe that every word in the original text was God-breathed. Words are important and fascinating. Never read so fast that you miss the words. Understanding of the meaning of a passage often depends on the understanding of a single word.

Objective: Use this lesson to stimulate interest in getting rich dividends from chapter, verse, and word study.

A Plan of Action

- Study by chapters
- Study by verses
- Study by words

Study by Chapters

1. Main subject

Most chapters of the Bible, in whole or in part, have a chain of development that emphasizes the main subject. It is our privilege to find this chain in a chapter. To find the chain we observe the links.

A chapter must be read until an outline is discovered. The main subject and principal lesson fastens upon our minds as we engage in prayerful reading and study. When studying, we should not leave a chapter until we have seen the development of some truth in it. Every chapter has some spiritual teaching for us. Wilbur M. Smith says:

> If a chapter does not have at least one great truth for us upon our first reading of it, then we ought to read it over again. If the time has gone for our devotional reading on any one day before the chapter has yielded some truth for our souls, then we can give it further thought while riding down to work on the streetcar, or walking to work, or as we go about the house in the normal duties of every day; and often by nighttime, we will find the chapter yielding some rich truths for our souls. If necessary, go back to the chapter the next day, or take the next chapter for a change and then go back to the earlier chapter a day or so afterwards, but do not let that particular passage in the Word remain for you a barren area: keep drilling through the soil and rock until you strike Living Water. My own experience has been that a chapter which involved the most thought, and which at first refused to give me anything, finally yielded up some spiritual teaching of unusual richness.

2. Prominent persons

Note the persons mentioned in the chapter. Pay attention to what is said about each one. If he is not well known, use a concordance to trace other references to him. In the Book of Philemon, verse 23, Epaphras is mentioned as Paul's fellow prisoner. A check will reveal two other references to him, both in Colossians (1:7; 4:12). From these verses we learn that he was a fellow prisoner, a dear fellow servant, and a faithful minister of Christ. Possessing "great zeal," but shut up in prison and no longer able to preach, he gave himself to the priestly work of intercession. His zeal found an effective outlet as he prayed "always," "fervently," and with a definite aim—that the Colossians and others "may stand perfect and complete in all the will of God" (Col. 4:12).

3. Key verse

Try to find the main verse, a key to the chain of truth in the chapter.

4. Other important points to look for

Find the commands to obey, the errors to avoid, the lessons to be learned, the promises to claim, and the prayers to use as patterns. How does the chapter relate to the great theme of the Bible—Christ and His redemption? How does it relate to the rest of the book?

Make a note of words significantly recurring in the passage. Are there expressions peculiar to the chapter and to the book? Check the meaning of words not understood.

5. Summary

The above items indicate three general rules for chapter study: 1) relate the chapter to its context; 2) find the links in its chain of development; and 3) make personal application of the truths revealed.

Example of Chapter Study

Psalm 119 is devoted to the grand theme—the Bible, the Word of God. This particular chapter is not difficult to analyze, as some chapters are.

This psalm, the longest chapter in the Bible and located in the very center, has been variously called "the alphabet of divine love," "the school of the truth," "a garden of meditations on the Word of God," "the storehouse of the Holy Spirit," "the epitome of all true religion," and "the Christian's golden ABCs of the praise, love, power, and use of the Word of God."

One of the most interesting things about this psalm is that every verse speaks of the Word of God; wherever we turn we find "the law," "the testimony," "the commandment," "the precept." Each verse of Psalm 119 is a glorious testimony to the beauty, power, and majesty of God's eternal Word, repeated 176 times over. Each of these verses seems to reflect a particular character of the Word. All are given that we may have God's holy and perfect Word engraved upon the panel of our hearts. This blessed "Word psalm" has 176 arrows searching us out and bringing a message to us. The Word is eminent and central throughout.

Let us notice some specifics from the riches of this psalm that is at the very heart and center of the Bible.

I. *The eternal character of the Word:* There are three outstanding statements that contain the word forever.
   A. *Forever settled*—"For ever, O Lord, thy word is settled in heaven" (v. 89). This is present tense truth.

    B. *Forever founded*—"Concerning thy testimonies, I have known of old that thou hast founded them for ever" (v. 152). This refers to the past tense—a foundation laid.

    C. *Forever enduring*—"Thy word is true from the beginning: and every one of thy righteous judgments endureth for ever" (v. 160). This is the assurance for the future. "The grass withereth, the flower fadeth: but the word of our God shall stand for ever" (Isa. 40:8). "Heaven and earth shall pass away: but my words shall not pass away" (Luke 21:33).

II. *The truth of the Word:* A triad is given us about the truth of the Word.

    A. *True from the beginning*—"Thy word is true from the beginning" (v. 160).

    B. *The Word is truth*—"Thy law is the truth" (v. 142).

    C. *All the Word is truth*—"Thou art near, O Lord; and all thy commandments are truth" (v. 151). The Bible is without error.

III. *The value of the Word:* God's Word provides cleansing, joy, comfort, song, riches, food, light, hope, and peace.

    A. *Cleansing*—"Wherewithal shall a young man cleanse his way? by taking heed thereto according to thy word....Thy word have I hid in mine heart, that I might not sin against thee" (vv. 9, 11).

    B. *Joy*—"Thy testimonies also are my delight and my counsellors" (v. 24).

C. *Comfort*—"This is my comfort in my affliction: for thy word hath quickened me" (v. 50).

D. *Song*—"Thy statutes have been my songs in the house of my pilgrimage" (v. 54).

E. *Riches*—"The law of thy mouth is better unto me than thousands of gold and silver" (v. 72).

F. *Food*—"How sweet are thy words unto my taste! yea, sweeter than honey to my mouth!" (v. 103).

G. *Light*—"Thy word is a lamp unto my feet, and a light unto my path" (v. 105). "The entrance of thy words giveth light; it giveth understanding unto the simple" (v. 130).

H. *Hope*—"Thou art my hiding place and my shield: I hope in thy word" (v. 114).

I. *Peace*—"Great peace have they which love thy law: and nothing shall offend them" (v. 165).

IV. *Rules for studying the Word*

A. *Approach the Word with prayer*—"Open thou mine eyes, that I may behold wondrous things out of thy law" (v. 18). Do this and these things will result:

1. *Our hearts will love to study the Word*—"Incline my heart unto thy testimonies" (v. 36).

2. *We will receive understanding*—"Give me understanding, that I may learn thy commandments" (v. 73). "I have more understanding than all my teachers: for thy testimonies are my meditation. I

understand more than the ancients, because I keep thy precepts" (vv. 99–100).

3. *We will be moved to awe by the Word*— "My heart standeth in awe of thy word" (v. 161).

4. *We will find great joy in study*—"I rejoice at thy word, as one that findeth great spoil" (v. 162).

B. *Meditate upon the Word*—"I will meditate in thy precepts, and have respect unto thy ways" (v. 15). We are instructed seven times in this psalm to make God's Word our meditation (vv. 15, 23, 48, 78, 97, 99, 148).

1. *We are to meditate on the Word at all times*—"O how I love thy law! it is my meditation all the day" (v. 97).

2. *By meditation comes knowledge*—"I have more understanding than all my teachers: for thy testimonies are my meditation" (v. 99; cf. Josh. 1:8; Ps. 1:2; 1 Tim. 4:15).

C. *Obey the Word*—"Blessed are the undefiled in the way, who walk in the law of the Lord. Blessed are they that keep his testimonies, and that seek him with the whole heart. They also do no iniquity: they walk in his ways. Thou hast commanded us to keep thy precepts diligently" (vv. 1–4).

These three rules affect the entire man—spirit, soul, and body. Prayerful study speaks of fellowship of the human spirit with God; meditation is the work of the mind and soul; obedience is the answer of the body.

Study by Verses

Many Christians give testimony to the blessing received from a single Bible verse. Some of the richest truths and helps for Christian living are found in some single verse that stands out above all others in morning devotions. All day long the Holy Spirit uses it to strengthen the heart, inspire the life, fortify against temptation, and stimulate for service.

Someone has suggested that if one verse is memorized each day for six days, and then the verses learned are reviewed on the seventh day, we would learn over three hundred verses a year. When learning a verse, meditate upon it, analyze it, take it apart, and put it together again. Study the verse in relation to its context. Then find the chain of thought.

The key to the understanding of any sentence lies in understanding the verbs. The spiritual meaning rests upon the exact force of the leading word or words. To understand the intent of the writer, let us ask what the sentence does or demands to be done.

Note the following lesson in letting the verbs speak. For the sake of having usual construction of a simple English sentence, liberty has been taken in rewording the sentences. The expressions *I have* and *I will* appear in a series of verses (Ps. 119:7–16). If we do those things expressed in the present perfect tense *(I have),* we can experience those listed in the future tense *(I will).* There are four "I haves" and six "I wills."

(Because) I have sought thee (v. 10),
I will praise thee (v. 7).

165

(Because) I have hid thy word (v. 11),
    I will keep thy statutes (v. 8);
    I will meditate in thy precepts (v. 15).

(Because) I have declared thy judgments (v. 13),
    I will delight myself in thy statutes (v. 16);
    I will not forget thy word (v. 16).

(Because) I have rejoiced in the way of thy tes-
    timonies (v. 14),
    I will have respect unto thy ways (v. 15).

Study by Words

There is a wealth of meaning hidden in the words of
the Bible. The more we study the Bible, the greater
will be our interest in its words and their meanings.
Every word in the original text is God-breathed.
Correct understanding of the Bible comes through
correct understanding of the words that the
Scriptures use.

Among the numberless proofs of Bible unity and
correctness, note the passage in Isaiah 9:6: "For unto
us a child is born, unto us a son is given." This is a
completely accurate statement. The Child was born,
but the Son was never born. He was eternal and
eternally a part of the Godhead. Christ was the
eternal Son, the Word. But He was born a child in
His incarnation.

Return to the chapter outline of Psalm 119. Read
once more the statements containing the word *forever.* The expression "for ever...settled" comes from
a Hebrew root signifying that it has been set up; it
stands upright. The word is occasionally used to

define a pillar. In other words, the Word, "for ever ... settled," stands upright, unshaken, and eternal.

The phrase "founded ... for ever" is translated from a Hebrew word meaning "to lay a foundation." It is the word used of the founding of the earth (Ps. 24:1–2; Prov. 3:19).

Much blessing can be received by tracing the usage of certain words by various writers. The word *precious,* used by Peter, brings a rich outline of spiritual truth:

We are redeemed by the "precious" blood of Christ (1 Pet. 1:19). We have obtained like "precious" faith as the redeemed (2 Pet. 1:1). The trial of our faith is more "precious" than that of gold that perishes (1 Pet. 1:7). We can find victory through trial because we have received great and "precious" promises (2 Pet. 1:4). Best of all, we believe upon Him who is "precious," literally, "the preciousness" (1 Pet. 2:6–7). The word indicates *essential preciousness,* that which is held in honor.

Illustrative and Practical

Figures of speech are often embedded in the common tongue of the Bible writer. Consider some of the figures of speech common to us today, which find their roots in the Bible—David and Goliath, the walls of Jericho, Gideon's three hundred, the land of Goshen, the cave of Adullam, the river Jordan, whited sepulchre.

Trace the origin of the following figures of speech: "they toil not, neither do they spin"; "the wrath of God"; "the handwriting on the wall"; and "I wash my hands of it."

167

Bible Facts

Item	Old Testament	New Testament	Total
Books	39	27	66
Chapters	929	260	1,189
Verses	23,214	7,959	31,173
Words	529,439	181,253	773,692
Letters	2,728,100	838,380	3,566,480

The middle chapter and the shortest in the whole Bible is Psalm 117. The middle verse is Psalm 118:8.

The middle book of the Old Testament is Proverbs. The middle chapter is Job 29. The middle verses are 1 Chronicles 29:17–18. The shortest verse is 1 Chronicles 1:25. Ezra 7:21 contains all the letters of the English alphabet except "j." Zephaniah 3:8 contains all the letters of the Hebrew alphabet. Two chapters are almost identical—2 Kings 19 and Isaiah 37.

The middle book of the New Testament is 2 Thessalonians. The middle chapters are Romans 13 and 14. The middle verse is Acts 17:17. The shortest verse is John 11:35.

The word *Jehovah* occurs 6,855 times in the Old Testament. The word *and* occurs 35,543 times in the Old Testament and 10,684 times in the New.

The oldest parable in the world is found in Judges 9:8–15.

Quick Quiz

- Do chapter and verse divisions appear in the original text of the Bible?

- What should a person look for in a chapter to get a proper understanding and receive spiritual blessing?

- Why are Bible words important?

- How can verses and words become meaningful to us?

Read

Psalm 138:2
John 5:39
2 Timothy 3:16–17
2 Peter 1:19–21

12

You and Your Bible

The Bible is a stream in which an elephant can swim and a lamb can wade.

Preview: Every Christian should know his Bible, and we believe every Christian can know his Bible. Many say that they do not have time for Bible reading, but they find time for other reading, which shows desire enters largely into the matter. It is safe to assume that if a Christian desires to know his Bible, he can. Bible study by an individual hinges on time, place, and method. Several lessons have been devoted to the principles of procedure outlined for method of study. The decision for time and place rests squarely with the individual.

True Bible study is more than study purely from the standpoint of the intellectual apart from the spiritual. There are many who examine the Bible academically and critically, refusing to take either its claims or its commands seriously.

The Christian approach is altogether different. The child of God turns to the Bible as a babe turns to his mother's breast, seeking nourishment and strength. It is his heavenly Father's Word and is as necessary to the spiritual body as physical food is necessary for the natural body. Realizing that man cannot live by bread alone, he yearns for "every word that proceedeth out of the mouth of God" (Matt. 4:4).

Objective: We must constantly and faithfully study the Bible to apply its teachings to our own spiritual lives and to learn how to use the Word in our ministry to others.

S–earching and receiving
T–rained and assured
U–nashamed and working
D–ividing and discerning
Y–ielding and heeding

God's Word Summarized

This Book reveals
the mind of God,
the state of man,
the way of salvation,
the doom of sinners, and
the happiness of believers.
Its doctrines are holy,
its precepts are holy,
its histories are true, and
its decisions are immutable.
READ IT to be wise,
BELIEVE IT to be safe, and
PRACTICE IT to be holy.
It contains:
LIGHT to direct you,
FOOD to support you, and

COMFORT to cheer you.
It is the traveler's map,
the pilgrim's staff,
the pilot's compass,
the soldier's sword,
and the Christian's character.
Here
Paradise is restored,
Heaven is opened, and
the gates of hell are disclosed.
CHRIST is its grand subject,
OUR GOOD is its design, and the
GLORY OF GOD is its end.
It should
fill the memory,
rule the heart, and
guide the feet.
Read it
slowly,
frequently, and
prayerfully.
It is
a mine of wealth,
a paradise of glory,
and a river of pleasure.
It is
given you in life,
will be opened at the Judgment,
and will be remembered forever.
It
involves the highest responsibility,
rewards the greatest labor,
and condemns all who trifle with its holy contents.

You can experience more of God's grace & love!